# Songs from a
# Lead-Lined Room

 Songs from a

# Lead-Lined Room

NOTES—HIGH AND LOW—FROM MY JOURNEY
THROUGH BREAST CANCER AND RADIATION

SUZANNE STREMPEK SHEA

BEACON PRESS, BOSTON

Beacon Press
25 Beacon Street
Boston, Massachusetts 02108-2892
www.beacon.org

Beacon Press books are published under the auspices of
the Unitarian Universalist Association of Congregations.

06  05  04  03  02    8  7  6  5  4  3  2  1

This book is printed on acid-free paper that meets
the uncoated paper ANSI/NISO specifications for
permanence as revised in 1992.

Text design by *George Restrepo*
Composition by *Wilsted & Taylor Publishing Services*

Library of Congress Cataloging-in-Publication Data
Shea, Suzanne Strempek.
    Songs from a lead-lined room : notes—high and low—from my
journey through breast cancer and radiation / Suzanne Strempek Shea.
        p. cm.
        ISBN 0-8070-7246-X
    1. Shea, Suzanne Strempek—Health. 2. Breast—Cancer—
Patients—United States—Biography. I. Title.
        RC280.B8 S4923 2002
        362.1'9699449'0092—dc21
                                        2001006234

This is dedicated to the late *Bruce MacMillan*,

founder of Broadside Bookshop in Northampton, Massachusetts.

The world that he worked to better misses him so.

# ❧ 1 ❧

My new guru has an office on the deep-down floor of the big hospital.

The walls here are yards thick and they are lined fat with lead. There is bad stuff being dealt with here, and it needs to be contained —not just the danger that people who come here are carrying inside themselves, but also the things that are aimed at them down here to try to kill that danger. Everything here is bad. Even the radio reception. Only one station can be caught through the fortress walls and it's lousy. *Lion King*. Disco revival.

The guru's room is the size of a car. A budget rental. Two chairs, and a shelf for a desk. Today she has offered me the option of having our session observed by an intern. This hospital is a teaching place, so at least one student in on an appointment or exam or procedure is not uncommon. Since late winter, in the name of education, dozens of strange hands have been placed on one of my more private areas. I'd get probed, and then thanked, and then later they'd see me in the hall with my clothes on and they wouldn't even nod a greeting. Kind of like high school. The weird thing about today is that it seems odder to have a stranger in on the listening than the touching. But I don't mind. I feel bad in my soul and at this point might even say yes to a live telecast.

The intern's name is Holly. It's bright, and, of course, holidayish. Holly wants to become a nurse and is attending Springfield College, so I compliment her because that is a fine school. She smiles from a face that belongs on a good-looking religious statue. Clear and open and ready for your prayers, and I wonder, in years to come will she turn out to be the kind of nurse who held my hand an hour past the end of her shift even though she really needed to get to the grocery before it closed. Or will she get burned-out and hateful like the one who shouted at me the time I asked again for a painkiller. You can't tell these things in advance, about how Holly, or anybody, might act in time. But for now, she shows every sign of being the type of nurse you'd want: interested, leaning in, but not getting in the way of my guru, Wendy, who knows what to say and when to shut up.

Wendy has not had this. I know because I asked, the first time I met with her as part of the package deal of radiation. If we have the inclination and time, we patients down here can be connected to helpful resources and activities that include a chaplain, massage therapists, reiki practitioners, meditation sessions, writing groups and art workshops. Colorful posters and leaflets hang in the waiting rooms and locker rooms, announcing the next series of courses. I was more in the mood to complain about my problems than to weave potholders. So I leaped at the chance for psychotherapy, and in Wendy found one of those huge iron posts to which they moor freighters at a dock. I was bobbing around, she was a possible line to stability. I connected with her right off, and right off I asked her: "Did you ever have this?" Knowing that was important to me. A lot of such things were—and are—important: top of the list, am I going to die from this? I'd asked that one three months earlier, of the nurse, on the phone the night I received my diagnosis. Cindy later said, "Wow, you asked that? I never thought to ask that." My best friend never thought to ask; even though her diagnosis eight years before had been dire. For me, despite the blessing of early detection and a classification of Stage One out of four, it was the first thing I wanted to know. You hear the word "cancer" and your name in the same sentence, and you can already see your name carved into the stone. At least I could.

So I needed to know if Wendy had personal knowledge of what she counseled people about while she sat all day in her tiny office on the deep-down floor of the hospital, doing her social work. She told me no, she'd never had it, but she went on to tell me she had known some of the forms of hardship that befall anyone who's alive, and I was all prepared to hear her go on and tell me about her cesarean, thinking she might be another of the surprising number of women who, when they learn about what's happened to me, scramble for a story to swap and start reciting, "Well, I went through fifty hours of labor only to have a cesarean." They got a child for all their misery, a bit more positive an experience than having mortality in your face, which is how the guru put it the first time we met. In your face. That's where it is with cancer. Of the fingernail, or of the brain. That's the thing. And even though Wendy has not had this, or any cesarean that she cared to mention, I felt she knew what she was talking about, and that she would help.

So I regularly will be going to see her in her office on the deep-down floor, where the waiting room is packed with people wondering what do you have and how bad is it? I should note, that is what I am wondering: what's he got? And what about her? A couple is sitting together, and you try to guess which one of them is the patient. Most of the people I see there are older. Some look terrible. But some look pretty good, and you have to remark about that, if only to yourself. One elderly man was showing off a diploma today. They actually give you a diploma when your treatments are over, which I think is a ridiculous thing. But this man apparently didn't. He appeared to be very proud. And, I have to say, he looked great. He didn't look sick. But then, I don't look sick. I don't feel sick. Yet I'm to be coming here five days a week for the next six and a half weeks, to get myself radiated while the theme from *The Lion King* plays and the technicians answer my fears by saying no, don't worry, this is not a dangerous thing being done to you here, and then they file from the room and shut the door and a red warning light beams from the ceiling so nobody will come back in until it's safe again.

This machine on which I am to be radiated is so old the technicians admit they don't even know its age. It is the dull tan color of the IBM Selectrics I used in the newsroom when I first worked as a reporter. Like the Selectrics, it is worn and scratched. But unlike a typewriter, it takes up an entire end of a room and has a moving arc-shaped part that curves around your body to the sound of a compressor, and if you were claustrophobic you might have trouble here. There is a new high-tech machine at the other end of the hall and there is to be an open house next week to show it off to the public. I have been given a laser-printed invitation to this event, which will include refreshments, and I ask if this means I will be treated on the newer model. No, I'm told, it is for dealing with parts found only in men. The cobalt machine—mine—does what's needed for me, I'm assured, has done the job for women for who knows how many years, and certainly will for my six and a half weeks. Maybe so, but to look at my machine, you'd think the power source was a crank and a pair of hamsters on a treadmill. Somebody has stuck pictures onto the part that encircles you. Transfers, the kind that people once dipped in water and applied to their kitchen walls. Two cardinal birds, both boldly red males, sit on a pine branch. A big pink flower blossoms nearby. These are supposed to cheer you, I guess. They don't work.

I feel rotten, I tell Wendy afterward, back in her little office with Holly in a chair she's jammed into the corner behind the door. I am worn out and defeated and I don't want to be coming to this hospital or anywhere near this hospital and I'm not happy that it's going to take no less than three weeks for the country's number-one antidepressant to kick in and give me a leg up and over the wall. I don't want to have cancer. I don't like having cancer. I turn to Holly even though the deal is I'm supposed to be pretending she isn't there. I tell her this has been going on for way too long, in my opinion. Since March. Fucking March. And here it is, September. Annual mammogram at the tail end of winter—what's this here? Another appointment to find out—no, that was nothing after all. But can you come back so we can take a look at the other breast?

≈≈

I'm forty-one and in the best physical shape of my life. Or so I thought. Go down the waiting room–posted list of preventative measures, and I've met them all. Because I thought my parents would kill me, I never once smoked. Or inhaled. Anything. Because I love being outdoors, I walk daily, in all weather. Because I woke up to the cruelty involved, I stopped eating meat more than a decade ago. Because it doesn't take much, I don't drink much. I was happy without having to force it. If this counts for anything, I went to church, I gave to charities, I packed groceries at the local food pantry, I recycled, I captured and released any bugs found in the house. I even bought the postal service's special breast cancer postage stamps, despite their costing seven cents more than the regular kind. Nothing's perfect, but I was in a life that always had made me feel lottery-lucky. I didn't squander that—I took care. I have no family history of the disease, but since age thirty-three faithfully have been going for mammograms due to a benign cyst discovered the same exact month Cindy was diagnosed. And about which, due to my guilt over escaping away free that time, I did not tell her until this year. Until my own bad news. Eight years back, though, from the unscathed side of our parallel universes, I watched her fight for her life. And I guess I have never stopped fearing for my own.

So at end of this past winter, I went for my usual look-see and was asked to return. And to come back again. There were more examinations for me. More mammograms in a single day than there are $m$'s in the word. An ultrasound in May. An extremely uncomfortable three-hour stereotactic core biopsy in June, my left breast dangling through a hole in a raised table while, seated below like a car mechanic working on a rattling muffler, a radiologist drilled repeatedly for samples.

Then it's the Fourth of July and we are visited by this blowhard guy and his wife and his two little kids, all of them out from Ohio. They lived here long ago, they knew my husband Tommy then, they always had meant to visit on trips back. And finally here they are in my home and I don't know any of them and I don't want to know any of them and I don't want them to be there and the night is dragging and the wife is nice enough but the guy won't shut up about downloading music from the Internet and when I finally find something to insert into the conversation, the name of an album I'd been listening to recently, he says, "Oh, you just heard of them?" The "just" is big, the size of a movie screen on which can be shown a film of my general lack of knowledge of what is hip. The kids don't care who knows what. They are restless and want to run in the rain that is pouring and when their parents say they cannot, they shout how they hate them and even though I don't know them I hate them, too, and I'm just begging them in my head to get out my house and leave me alone because tomorrow I'll be told what I've got or not got growing in what the clinic's paperwork maps out as the upper left quadrant of my left breast.

The family eventually leaves, of course, and the next day arrives, of course. And, of course, the call does not come anywhere as swiftly as I would like. I'm waiting all the day and on the hour I'm pestering the nurse on the line, she says the doctor's in surgery and I'm thinking how it's an awful long operation already, taking this many hours —somebody must have something really bad that needs repair. I pray for whoever it is. I've always liked to pray for strangers. They'll never know. It's as if you're sending something out there, invisible, unexpected, the source unknown if the beneficiary ever did stop to wonder why things maybe ended up the way they were hoping. Powerful stuff it can be. But I don't pray for myself on this day. And I haven't since, even though I have spent much of my life begging daily for favors, most of them for me me me. The instinct to do that has vanished. Lots of things have fallen away in these months and don't seem to matter, and I wonder if they ever will.

I have a basket of get-well cards, the wicker almost dissolving from the sweetness of the messages. Everybody offers to take up the slack of the praying for favors. I don't even know some of these people. I am on actual lists at local churches, my name typed under the heading of "sick" and placed at the feet of the statues of saints known for their great batting averages in interceding. I've not personally seen any of these lists, and I don't want to. I don't look sick. I don't feel sick. Why should my name be on a list that says I am? I go to the CVS to pick up the country's number-one antidepressant and a stranger stops me to ask what's wrong with me—her whole entire church is praying for me and she wants to know: "What's wrong?" Other than "Who are you?"—which I do not reply—I don't know what to answer. I just shrug, "Oh, well, things. . . ." but I would like to add that maybe the praying should have begun a little earlier. Like three months before, on the fifth of July, when I was waiting for the doctor to phone me. Tenth call to his office. Last few times, the nurse has been saying yes, yes, she has the results now, but only the doctor can give them out. So I ask her this: if it was good news, would I have to wait for the doctor to tell me? That gets her thinking, and even though she prefaces how it is against the rules, she reads me the results. I have Cindy's medical book in front of me. I'm looking up the words as the woman is giving them to me.

≈≈

My fifty minutes are up. Holly will be able to do an entire term paper now. I repeat to her face that I don't want this—what's happened so far in these six months and what is to come. The prognosis is good, I realize things could be much worse, but it's happening to me. And that makes it bad enough. I slide from feeling as if I'm whining to feeling justified about the whining, then back again, sometimes with Olympian luge speed. I whoosh unprotected down the icy incline of helplessness and unknowing, no sled beneath me, no snowsuit padding, no clothing at all, no cap or mittens or boots, no nothing, no skin even, it's like my bones are showing, I feel so down to the base of whoever I am, more naked than the moment I was conceived, feeling everything. Same time, feeling nothing.

"I just don't want this," is how I condense all that. And however Holly views this, she doesn't let on. Wendy does, though, and she asks, "Well, what do you want?" which is a good question, both right then or anytime.

I tell her this:

"I just want my life back the way it was."

⌁⌁

My life.

I liked it.

I liked it the way it was.

I had it good, and was smart enough to realize that. To be grateful.

Well into adulthood, I still held the practice of evening prayers, still moving through a trio I've said in my family's native Polish, long ago having hitched a list on to the end of them. Last thing, in the silent dark, I'd name three experiences, feelings, items, thoughts from my day, things that made me grateful. And I would reflect on them. Watch them like a movie. Remember the emotions they brought: a kindness shown to me. Unexpected breaks. The solution to a trouble that had been hanging over me. Spotting a face I love to see. Opening a check arriving from nowhere. Finding a full sack of Cool Ranch Doritos unopened in the cabinet. Reaching the answering machine, rather than the actual person, when I didn't really want to have to talk to that person in the first place. Often, one of the three things would string into dozens of others. In January, I'd hear the rush of air from the furnace and would be grateful to have a furnace. And money for the oil to fire it—a tank full of that, and a basement to put the tank in and a house on top of that basement, a house that was mine, filled with my immediate loves: the man, the dog, the space in which to do my work. Outside my window, a roof of trees, a carpet of grass and flowers, the smoothly paved road to fantastic adventures yet unknown.

Throughout my early years my grandparents gave me the usual grandchildren gifts of savings bonds and graduation watches, but they also unknowingly handed me this capacity to realize my fortunate place in the wild, capricious and enormous scheme of things. Many people do not have the ability to pinpoint exactly who planted their families in this country. For most of my first two decades on earth, I could look across a kitchen table and see first generation Americans living and breathing and drinking a cup of tea. One pair of my grandparents lived downstairs in our two-family house as I was growing up. The other was half an hour west. For years they populated birthdays and vacation trips, Easter mornings and Christmas Eves, and so many of the regular days in between. One grandmother lived to see me into college. The other, long enough to read my regular byline in her evening paper.

Not once can I recall any of them hanging over my head the weight of the smallest debt I owed them. No litanies of how they'd struggled and sacrificed, working in mills, running a restaurant, all so their children, and their children's children—including me—could succeed. In fact, they made little if any fuss about what they had done to get to this country, and to prosper in comfortable middle-class status. Instead, it was their proximity, their physical presence, that nurtured in me a recurring gratitude for the life that, through them, I felt blessed to lead.

One grandparent was an infant when she arrived, but three others were teens striking out alone. Imagine. My own teenage years contained no concern larger than whether I was going to miss the school bus each morning. My existence was carefree. I had friends, and we had fun. I made Bs in school and, after dismissal, grinders at the Food Basket.

I rode my bike. I walked in the woods. I went on dates. I went to the mall, to the beach. I had a mother and a father who loved me and who provided my sister and me everything necessary, plus bonus stuff like camping trips and pets and Earth Shoes. And higher education. Though I went to art school and studied photography, I fell into writing and found work that I not only could do, but liked to do and needed to do. Work that many days was not work but something else—a rare, true enjoyment. I genuinely looked forward to going into the newsroom during my fifteen years as a reporter, always something new to learn, no two days the same. One beat had me venturing into the locker rooms of sports teams, another had me seated next to a small-town dog officer while he proffered photographic proof of a canine's regular soiling of town property. On yet another beat, I'd spend a couple of weeks in New York City each spring and fall, once taking notes next to a fidgety Andy Warhol, while models wearing the latest fashions paraded down a design studio's runway. Beginning a night shift at the end of the eighties, I found my mornings suddenly free. I'm most creative at that time and wondered what I would do during the hours in which I usually was making stories for someone else. I decided to make some for myself. And to make them up. To try writing fiction.

The experience of not having to quote people exactly, to throw aside fact and play with scenarios, all of it was heady. And fun. I didn't write my first short story with the hope that I would get a huge contract and be able to leave my job. I wrote it because it was a hoot. I sent a few short stories to magazines, and I got a few rejections, which actually made me feel more like a writer than the act of putting a story on a page. And then my third story grew way beyond the dozen-page constraints the others had fit into, and I saw no end in sight. Tommy saw something else: the start of a new kind of writing for me.

We'd met when I was a hockey-loving high schooler and he was a sportswriter who never once mentioned my team in his stories. I wrote him a nasty note, he corrected his ways, I went to thank him and took note of the fact he was cute. And when I leaned close to say something he couldn't hear over the crowd noise, I was struck by how he smelled like home to me. He became the best friend I'd ever had, and ten years later we married. Seven years after that, in 1991, I was writing a very long short story and Tommy was a general assignment reporter who'd just interviewed Elinor Lipman, a local author with a national reputation. He bragged about my sixty-page "short" story; this stranger was kind enough to offer to read it, and ended up sending it to an agent friend who sent it to an editor. Their encouragement fueled the sixty pages to become a manuscript, the manuscript became a book, the fiction writing became my new job.

Zooming in on my life from a satellite in 1999, the year before I was diagnosed with breast cancer, you would have seen me snug in my own little world, living in the town where I was raised, next to Tommy not only in domestic life, but at a long white desk at which we wrote daily at our respective computers, he now working on his thrice-weekly newspaper column, me on my fourth novel. I was looking to the publication of the paperback of my third, that one about an artist who collects the people who've become family as true as the one into which she'd been born. The concept was something I knew well, and was another thing I was grateful for, the gemlike ring of sisters and brothers I'd been fortunate enough to draw into my life story along the way. Though much of their presence was often necessary and reassuring, I always had a level desire to be all I needed. Comfortable with time alone, I even used it as a celebration. I'd turned forty on my last birthday and, being an avid walker, gave myself an eight-day trek in Ireland. Most of the route, I saw no other humans. Alone, solitary, I was also content. It was all right with me.

Like most people, I carried my kit of challenges as I moved along the path of life. Except for getting coughed on by a neighbor girl when I was an infant just home from the hospital and, according to family lore, contracting pneumonia in that way, and except for getting my face smashed into the windshield when the family Plymouth Fury III ran into a tree a dozen years later, the injuries I suffered were mainly to my soul. I did my share of running headfirst into the universal brick walls of confusion, rejection, disappointment, loss. I was called sensitive, and even being labeled that was painful, despite being the truth. Though the nuns trooped us from the parish school to the church next door to beef up attendance at more than a few sparsely attended parish funerals over my eight years of education there, my first meaningful introduction to mortality was at age nine, the loss of my beloved downstairs grandfather, who fell to the green paisley living room carpet in a sudden heart attack on a regular Friday night with all the family over for dinner and me there complete with my sleepover guest. Determined to be too impressionable to attend a funeral—a decision I did not fight—I spent that day wearing my sister's coveted red, white and blue tennis V-neck as I minded a family friend's toddler child who was a terror then and is now a fashion model and sportscar salesman out in California.

My grandfather's death coated me long after the actual incident; for the endless months that followed, my aunts' and uncles' regular Sunday visits downstairs included adults who actually wept at some point in the afternoon, something I'd never before witnessed. I remember sitting on my grandfather's bed trying to console an uncle slumped there in his grief. I put my hand on the shoulder of his white dress shirt and listened to him choking out something about regret and I wondered what was happening to my happy little world. Mine was not a touchy-feely family, and it was left up to me to figure this out, to wade through and come to terms with my loss. For years I'd covered my head with my bedpillow to escape the excruciating sound of my grandfather's asthmatic breathing from his room below mine. While I matched my strong inhalations to his labored ones in an effort of support, I told myself he was sounding better when I knew he was getting worse. What I eventually gleaned from losing my grandfather was: even if you can see it coming as clear as the Canadian National freight train that flew down the tracks behind my neighborhood each morning at two, when old people die, if you happen to love them, it hurts.

Fourteen years later I was dressing for work when a woman from up the street phoned to tell me that her niece—my best and oldest friend—

had been killed in a horrific auto accident. Rosemary had just begun her first real job, just out of graduate school, just back from our shared three weeks of joyous holiday roaming around California, and she was driving to buy herself an iron, and there was a car then a truck then another truck and she was gone.

In a way, I was gone as well. Jarred off the map of what I knew to be my safe and cozy life. Rosemary was buried for eternity in the red and blue floral dress she'd bought for job interviews, and I was shuffling around in the same jeans and flannel shirt day after day because I couldn't be bothered to care about looking presentable. I was as much in shock as if I'd been next to her in the front seat of her new gray Escort. I learned from this that you can be young and die, too. You can be my same age, and be gone in a hair of an instant. The thing people said about life being short—I suddenly saw it imprinted upon every moment of the day. I took the legend seriously, and soon I was unable to pass up the most last-minute social invitation from the least-known acquaintance. Two of Rosemary's other friends and I rented a lakefront A-frame for the summer and rarely were just the three of us there, its cavernous living room and the wraparound deck just begging to be the site of continuous partying. By the end of that summer, I'd purchased my own little A-frame in another set of woods on another lake, because that was the type of place I'd always wanted to have, the kind of place I'd always wanted to live in, and I'd better do it now because after all, really and truly, look at what happened to Rosemary: I could be gone by the end of this very day.

I moved along, bearing that realization, seeing it constantly as if written on a pane of glass behind which I walked. Life is short. Life is short. I knew that. Oh, I was so smart, I knew what others, untouched by such an experience, could not even imagine. Then, ten years later I'm on my driveway and Cindy is moving toward me, her husband David behind her, both of them walking in film slow-motion from their van to tell me the results of her doctor's appointment. That thing she thought was swelling after all her yardwork? Breast cancer. At age thirty-four. She would undergo a mastectomy. What were they going to tell their three kids? Could they sit in my house while they figured that out?

I needed to sit, too. Cindy long ago had slipped into the tender heartspot that Rosemary had occupied. It was Rosemary who introduced me to Cindy, who lived on her street, was a year older than we were, went to public school while most of the kids in Rosemary's and my world were ensconsed in our parish one. Cindy was twelve or so when I first met her, a tiny thing with long straight white-blonde hair and wire-rimmed glasses, a perfect Jan Brady stand-in. She had her own bedroom and a big family and an Eskimo dog. She got me my first summer job, in eighth grade, following a mentally challenged kid through his day of swimming and making soda-bottle bird feeders at the local Y camp until I caught mononucleosis despite not yet having been kissed and then slept until September. Her parents let Cindy have parties and she hosted a surprise one for my sixteenth, shoving Tommy in through the kitchen door as the biggest surprise. She and Rosemary and I rode our bikes to watch her brother's cross country team charge from the starting line and sweatily return an hour or so later; we walked endless miles up and down our do-nothing Main Street, slept at the beach in a little red pop-up tent, but only after she'd gone in to scout for the spiders I abhorred. Cindy married early on and I didn't see her much for a couple years after that, but she was the first person I phoned when I was told about Rosemary. Instinctively I went to Cindy, and had grown closer than ever in the ten years that led up to that day in August when she came to me with her news of cancer. Sure, my house was on the way home from the hospital. But, still, she came to me.

Three months later, I'm on the couch sketching camels for that year's Christmas card. Three of them doing their slow metronome plodding toward a star. I like to make my own cards, was thinking I'd print these with a potato so I was keeping the details to a minimum as potatoes aren't good for capturing fine lines. Phone rings and it is the hospital. The woman wants to know, was I Edward's daughter? She says there's been an emergency. That I should come right over.

My father went as my grandfather had. Heart attack. Two months after retirement, with all those plans for all that free time. Stricken while he was in my old bedroom recuperating from a stubborn ankle sprain. I was Edward's daughter. And also his biggest fan. And someone suddenly crushed flat.

The words that had been dangling in front of me for a decade now suddenly had an addendum: you can be older but in relative good health, and still die. I picked myself up again, this time with a new hard-earned enlightenment: don't wait until retirement. Be here now.

At my father's wake and funeral, Cindy wore a black velvet chapeau that would have seemed the height of fashion if you didn't know that she was using it to keep her chemotherapy-balded head warm in the early winter. She was tinier than ever, but she held me up. Tommy on one side, she on the other.

I know well that everybody loses somebody; some people even lose a whole lot of somebodies. I line up mine only to underscore that a good portion of my life has been spent trying to make the most of my time—because I long have known what it was like to have death somewhere close enough to hear it breathing and shifting in its chair, and once in a while it would stand up and show off its muscles. But after I was diagnosed with a disease that correctly wears the banner of "killer," I felt that I'd only been playing at knowing that. It's one thing to feel increasing depths of concern when you hear that cancer has hit a public figure, the woman down the street, your best friend. I've received and reacted to all of the above news. But I found it's another thing entirely to have the diagnosed person be yourself. Of all the things that have happened in my life, good and bad, nothing has held this much power over me.

Early detection, a slow-growing tumor, otherwise fine health, highly recommended physicians and up-to-date health facilities—all those were on my side. Yet I found extremely jarring simply being told

I had cancer. This is a thing with a reputation for killing people. And it was inside me.

Me.

≈≋≈

That's me sitting next to Cindy on Sharon's couch in the early summer of 2000. That's Sharon on the other side of her. Sharon was Rosemary's lifelong neighbor, their ranchhouses next door to each other on Edgewood Street, around the corner from Cindy's on Barker. As was the case with Cindy, it was through Rosemary that I met Sharon, and she became another of the sisters I've collected, the first one with a wildfire of red hair and a similar incendiary spirit. This is a long-overdue get-together. Sharon and her Gary have a hot tub on their deck and we all were to have a soak, but rain forced us indoors. After wet pizza at the kitchen table, we moved to the living room and to some real talk. Sharon's brother had died the winter before, and in an attempt to be helpful I asked, "How are you doing about Scott?" Sharon shrugged, said she was keeping busy and how that was a good thing. I offered, "Why don't you write about how you're feeling now?" Her answer: "Why don't you?"

Right then, a few weeks after diagnosis, a couple before surgery, I couldn't. Maybe it was the thing about seeing the words on the screen in front of me, which would make my problem realer than it already was. Whatever was stopping me, it did. So rather than writing, I'd been reading. Books, pamphlets, magazine pieces, on-line information. The binder full of cancer-related material I received like some kind of "welcome to the club" gift upon my first visit to the surgical oncologist. I'd consumed a big basket of information so I could know as much as possible about this sudden and shocking enemy.

When surgery found no involvement of lymph nodes, which meant chemotherapy wouldn't be necessary and a huge Hollywood-style party could have been thrown for that fact alone, I learned I would be facing radiation treatments. At the hospital I was given a small booklet on the subject, but wanted more information. Searching bookstores, the Web, my local library, I found little to nothing about radiation. Call up the words in a database, and you get titles on Hiroshima and Chernobyl. Change your search to "radiation for cancer," and your options mostly are medical texts that, even if you wanted to read them, are priced at hundreds of dollars. Within breast cancer books the mentions of radiation are scant, and say roughly two things—the treatments might make you tired, and they might damage your skin. What about the entire experience of having daily treatments for a month and a half? What was that like? Was it so easy that it wasn't worth mentioning? Or so difficult that no writer knew where to begin?

Eventually I found out the answer. And wrote it myself, daily, in the entries that opened this book and in all those that follow. But I was unable to write a word until the first day I went to the radiation oncology department. The radiation oncologist—named Mary Ann just like my sister, and the doctor specializing in this treatment—likes you to "meet" the machine and wants to walk you through your visit before things actually begin. The technicians draw lines on your chest and also actually inject a dye that makes up the tattoo dots at the treatment field's borders. The September afternoon on which this took place, I returned home and took the advice Sharon had given three months before. I went straight to the computer. The words fell from me. I couldn't even tell Tommy about my first visit until I felt I'd written what I needed to. What follows here are diary entries centering around the radiation treatments I received at 3:30 P.M. every Monday through Friday for seven consecutive weeks from late September to early November in the year 2000.

I wrote them for myself. As therapy. I'm not a journal devotee. The only diary I ever regularly kept was back in 1967, and it chronicles only about seventeen days in the January following the Christmas I'd found it in my stocking. The four allotted lines per day kept reports brief, the only notable one being January 10's "Uncle Mitzi came over and we watched the beetles at Shay Statium." Obviously, I'd hung on to that little blue diary with the lock that never worked. As for the computer pages that contained what I wrote thirty-three years later, they initially were destined for the fire. I considered burning the pages when I was done writing, some effort toward whatever is that thing called closure. But first, I wanted Tommy to read them, in the hope they would help him better understand what my side of the experience had been like. I made a copy for Cindy as well, as she'd once again been propping me up from the other side. And I made one for my friend Padraig, who'd lent me a home in Ireland to which I went off to write once the treatments were through, the thought of such a trip being a carrot on the end of the stick throughout the seven weeks. All three encouraged me to share the pages with others, thinking this might help someone who'd been in my boots. I knew that reading another's experience in radiation would have assisted me with mine. And it is in that spirit that I write to patients, to their loved ones, to their health professionals, about my journey into, and out of, the lead-lined room.

## ❦ 2 ❧

I will sit in the interior waiting room now that I'm going to be a regular. It's down the hall from the main waiting room of the radiation oncology department and is a rectangular space with half a dozen chairs along each of the two walls. The ends of the room are open so you can proceed easily to your particular machine room, by way of either of the two hallways, when your name is called by the technician. There are square tables with reading lamps at the ends of the rows, and an assortment of the outdated *Times* and *Peoples* you find in any such place. On both long walls are prints of a watercolored flower. There also is a framed poster encouraging you to enjoy the simple things in life, and in case you can't come up with any while you are sitting in this waiting room, it offers you a list: a walk in the woods, ice cream, a cat. A rack of brochures holds English and Spanish versions of literature on cancer treatments, on support groups, on how to, despite your current state of body and mind, deal with insurance issues or have sexual relations. Information, recommendations, statistics. All the things I am starting to add to my brain file, facts I can rattle off at the slightest opening in conversation. That breast cancer is the most common form of cancer found in American women, that it is the second leading cause of cancer deaths for all women, and that it is the leading overall cause of death for women ages forty to fifty-five, the range into which I fall. In this year of 2000, 182,799 other American women will join me in being diagnosed—one every three minutes. Also this year, in this country alone, 40,800 women will die of it. One every thirteen minutes. One woman joining the ranks and one leaving, all in the time it takes me to walk one of my morning miles. In 1960, the national rate of breast cancer was one in fourteen. Thirty years later, it is one in nine.

When I was attending art school in Maine in the late 1970s, a radio commercial featured a popular local comedian commenting on the state's high rate of cancer. Something like one in three state residents would be affected by the disease in some form. The comedian's take on this was that whenever you're in Maine, and are in a room with two other people, find the door. Three decades later, I was two states south and I was the one in nine. And that's why I was in this waiting room this late September afternoon, for my second day of radiation prescribed in the wake of surgery the month before. Radiation kills cells good and bad, so you must heal somewhat before you go on to the treatments. I was asked to wait six weeks. And in this year of waiting, that was another lengthy gap between the miserable tired-of-it here and the scary-unknown there, between the first test or pronouncement or procedure, and the next. Waiting, I stuck close to home, feeling as I did after Rosemary, after my father. I was at once shocked, smacked in the face, my legs kicked from under me, keenly aware that the world was just too big and frightening and that if I were out in it, a variety of bad things could occur. So in the six weeks I waited to begin treatments, I didn't venture far, if I went anywhere at all. I circled the backyard like an inmate on recreation break. I waited tensely for Tommy to return from work, any tardiness translating into his being involved in a massive car crash. Once he got home, I'd hug him simply for being alive, then soon would pick my way into a quarrel for no reason other than nerves. Because I work at home, people know I'm almost always there, and during this time friends and family came and went with a love-fired frequency, often in overlapping drop-ins that made for odd groupings of personalities I'd never intentionally place in the same room. Gifts of chocolates and fruit and cookies, plants and flower arrangements materialized and were eaten or admired by the next wave of visitors. All of them told me I looked great, that they were happy to see me up and around, I didn't look sick, did I feel sick? Didn't I want to go for a walk? Or for a ride or to the store? Some days I fell into them as if their open arms were nets at the ground floor and I'd just found myself plummeting from the top of the Prudential Center. Other days I actually hid, ignoring the bell and the barking dog, scrambling up the stairs to be out of sight of those who, as some did, walked around the house to check on me through the first-floor windows. I often found I preferred—and needed—to stare at the wall and digest what had happened to me, what was still happening to me as the days until treatment dragged.

What is happening now is the newest phase, and the last, I trust, of what will be done to me. Finally receiving the radiation meant to kill any cancer cells that remained after the tumor was removed by lumpectomy, a surgical procedure crying out for a name that sounds less like something from a Dr. Seuss book. Today in the waiting room there is an old man, and a woman younger than he but older than I am. I keep noticing that I am the youngest person I see in any of these rooms. Something about that bothers me, like, maybe there has been some kind of mistake—I'm not supposed to be here, really. The old man puts down his magazine and goes looking for the nurse. I hear him in the hall, complaining rudely about how long he's been waiting, I hear the nurse telling him really loudly but kindly how she hasn't forgotten him, things are just backed up today, can he wait a bit? And, to be totally honest, because he's annoying me, I'm thinking, why is he even bothering with this? He looks ancient. At that age, would you even care that much about living longer? As for the woman who's waiting, she is jiggling her knees nervously. I'm trying to look into my book of short stories, but I can see this, how, just across from me, she's jiggling her knees. I also can hear her breathing, exasperated. I don't look up. She's maybe four feet across from me and I can't even bring myself to look at her face. I just keep reading the short story, about the little kid who wanted to stay later at his grandmother's, so his mother goes into the other room to take a rest and a truck rams through the wall of the bedroom and kills her. Someone recommended this book to me, and maybe a cheerier tale would be a better pick at this time. Yet despite the content, it doesn't sadden me. Mainly because, even though I'm trying to pretend I'm not, I'm paying more attention to the woman across the way.

In the fuzz of my peripheral vision, up from the story about the boy and the mother and the truck, I can see she's wiping at her eyes. What do you do in a case like this? What is the protocol? The old man, now returned from his griping and now three seats to the left of her, flips loudly through a *Popular Mechanics*. The woman is sniffling and I want to get up and tell her OK OK OK. But maybe she'll bat me away. "What do *you* know?" That's what I might say to her if the situation were reversed. How do *you* know it'll be OK? That's what I say in my head when people tell me this—don't worry, things'll be fine, you'll do great. Smile. Think good thoughts. It'll be OK. I've heard all that. I hate all that. This type of advice, often well-meaning, seems trite and unfeeling, and also doesn't come close to acknowledging the weight of what someone is carrying—whatever their situation. The sniffling woman's particular situation I actually know something about. And I'm finding it hard to not worry, to think things'll be fine, to wear a mask of something I don't feel inside. So I'm not going to suggest she do any of that, and I don't say anything to her. Instead, I read about the boy and his guilt about his mother and his running through the fields toward home while the woman across from me is busy brushing things from her shoes. They're black and ballet style and worn-out and they look too little for her feet. She works at them diligently. Then the nurse comes to the doorway and asks "Ready?" and I watch the shoes leave, in a hurry.

When I get called in for my turn, I lie on the bed part of the machine and put my head in the little dish as I'm supposed to and the technician there, Annette, asks how my day was, how I am since yesterday, my first treatment. I imagine she must ask this of everybody, some small question in an attempt to put patients at ease. I say, "Well, I found my way back here." And she says, "But you didn't want to, did you?" She asks this as if she knows. I tell her no, I didn't want to, but here I am. With my head in the hard little dish the size in which you would serve fruit salad, Annette moves aside the left flap of my front-opening hospital gown, takes my left arm and places it in the cuff above my head, adjusting my upper body beneath the red target beam coming down from the machine, just the way she did yesterday. "Here, I'm going to move you, don't help me." That's what she says—don't help me. If you help her by moving yourself, it is no help—she knows what she's doing and where she wants your body to be positioned. So I don't help her. I let her shift me. She slides me around a bit, using the sheet I'm on. She has a TV clicker-type control hanging from a fat wire and she's using that to make the machine descend so close to my face that I can hear the echo of my voice deaden. The room lights go out. Red target lines fall across the center of my chest, and I trace their path up through the air to a hole in the ceiling tiles. Don't help me. Annette adjusts some more. She pushes up against my scars. She apologizes and says she hoped that didn't hurt. I like her, so I say no. She wears a Claddagh ring on her pinkie, a pair of hands cradling a heart. Her blond hair is in ringlets the way you do up a little girl's for Christmas Eve. She has on pajama-ish surgical clothing, and sneakers that make silent steps as she leaves the room and shuts the door tightly and the red warning light starts up and the machine hisses and then falls silent as it does its work.

The process takes less than ten minutes. Five or so with the machine in one position, then Annette will come in and swing the arc over to the other side, and then leave again, and another five minutes of the treatment the literature tells me is received by more than half of all cancer patients. I don't know how all the others feel about it, but as I lie on the machine and stare at the acoustic ceiling tiles, from the one-station radio, the Pointer Sisters are sounding pretty happy singing that they're so excited they simply can't hide it, they're about to lose control, and they think they like it.

## ☙ 3 ❧

I'm driving down the pike and he's up on the Baptist Hill overpass, a man in a straw cowboy hat, butter-colored shirt snapped up to the neck, trousers roughly the same color. He's stocky and serious, leaning into the chain link that keeps people from falling down onto the roadway. He's got his hands level with his shoulders and his fingers are hooked through the wire, the way you might place them if there were somebody on the other side you really wanted to touch. As I pass beneath him, I give a little wave, just a small move of my fingers off the steering wheel. He doesn't respond. I check the rearview mirror— it would be something if he weren't there anymore, had disappeared, was just a vision I'm supposed to divine the meaning of during a time in my life when I'm constantly searching for a message. But, no, he's still there, the back of him, standing still.

As I enter the waiting room, there's the woman I couldn't look at yesterday. She moves fast, past me, into the locker room.

"I'm Jack, I'll be your technician today."

The guy who calls me into the hall and walks me to the machine room tells me this in a kind of restaurant-speak. Then somebody else comes into the room, maybe her name is Lucy. Where is Annette, I ask. She's out sick, they say. I tell them she didn't look sick. Then I realize I've met her only twice, how would I know what she's supposed to look like, good or bad? Annette is sick. I don't like this. What's she got, I wonder. But I don't ask.

"How was the Big E traffic today?" Jack wants to know this as he draws my gown open. The Big E—the region's largest country fair—has begun its annual nearly three-week run, and the roads are jammed. I answer, "Fine." Jack nods as he adjusts me and I don't help him. He is big and soft-looking and reminds me of the son of the woman who taught me accordion, a quiet kid who wore plaid shirts and always had his head down. Jack has his head down, but to look at the measurements. He makes the top part of the machine descend. If I move my eyes enough to the side, just to the point where that action makes me dizzy, I can see another decoration stuck to the beige metal. Some kind of little person seated on a crescent moon. I realize now that I have not yet looked at the entire machine. I go right to my space on it, and that's that. So when the treatment is over, I stand back and take it in, the thing shaped like a giant microscope and lurking there at the end of the room. I can't look at it for very long.

≈≈

"What happens in there?"

Now that I've begun the treatments, people are starting to ask me this.

Most of them women. And most of their ideas about radiation are strange.

"Do they make you stand up against the wall?"

More than one person has wondered this. I don't know where the firing-squad image comes from, but I keep hearing it. I say no, you don't stand against a wall. "Well, where do you stand?" I say that you don't stand anywhere. You lie down. "All day?" Ten minutes, I tell them. "Ten minutes?" They are incredulous. "What good is that going to do?" A nice seed to plant in my head, thank you.

They ask if the procedure hurts. I tell them it doesn't hurt, that I don't feel a thing. It's like having an X ray taken. And, except for a little vacuum-cleaner whooshing noise when the machine comes on, there is no noise at all. No feeling of anything. Just annoyance about the bad music being played. In fact, I'm thinking you could just put together some nonworking parts of machinery in your basement and advertise that you're giving radiation treatments. Get your patient settled beneath your contraption, exit the room for a bit and have a tea, come back in and they're done and you'll see them tomorrow—and charge an enormous fee, of course. In the far last room on the deep-down floor of the actual real hospital, I lie on the actual real machine and I don't see anything happening, I don't feel anything. It all must be taken on faith in invisible rays.

I have to admit that in advance I thought I'd be visiting a version of the orange-bulbed heat lamp suspended above the french fries at your local drive-through. I envisioned myself as a big order of Vidalia onion rings or a deep-fried Captain's Platter, lying—not standing, that didn't even cross my mind—in a heat-lamp experience. But there's no warmth once I remove my sweatshirt and open the gown. The table is cold, the room is cold, the music is bad—did I mention that?—I'm half naked in front of strangers plus a television camera. In the hall, Annette, or Jack, or Lucy, whoever's my person for the day, needs to see me on a TV monitor. Should I freak out or have a question, they will see me on the screen passing out or flailing and they'll come in to help. It crosses my mind that there probably is a live feed to some strange Website. So, this day, just after the point where I'm not supposed to move, I wave.

≈≈

I come home to find in my mail Saint Peregrine, the Patron Saint of the Sick. Diane, a friend living across town on evocatively named Baptist

Hill, has sent me this. In the painting on the card, he's got a big black robe on and a white cloth tied around his ankle. He doesn't look sick. But Jesus must know something we don't, because He is shown going to the great effort of coming down from the cross to see Peregrine. Little angels are flying everywhere, helping, propping up. Diane has sent Saint Peregrine along with a note that tells me how she went to the Big E and missed the chance to see the governor, but did catch a demonstration of an eight-hundred-dollar ironing board and iron and she points out she doesn't own that amount in clothing. She concludes with, "The parade at the fair had a team of six camels pulling a wagon. These animals made no sound as they walked down the street! Keep your spirits up!"

She writes these things all in a row, just like that.

# ❧ 4 ❧

The guru tells me I have a lot of fear.

Immediately, I feel see-through. Transparent like the plastic woman back in Mr. Cornwell's high school biology class, with nothing at all hiding what she bears inside. Early on in this, Wendy seems to know my interior, and that's unsettling. But then I feel better because she says, "I have a lot of fear, too."

Other than her cool fashion sense—animal-print vests, bold silver earrings, no-nonsense short hairdo—that's one of the things I like about this woman: you have something wrong with your mind, chances are she does as well. She doesn't come off as trying to be perfect. And if she has the same things wrong with her that I do, well, she's got to be normal, right? So I must be, too.

Holly, the nursing student, is there again. I notice she is official today, has a card hanging from a cord around her neck bearing her photo and name. I saw my own photo today. In the file they have at the technician's desk just outside the lead-lined room. The file folder was open, and I saw myself looking out from it, so I looked back. They take your photo when you arrive to meet the machine, I guess so they'll know who they're seeking in the waiting room. Also, I'd imagine, so they don't do something to the wrong person. In the black-and-white photo

I look stunned, as if you are coming at me with a car ninety miles an hour and I'm in the middle of the street minding my own business and just starting to take notice of your swift approach. I remember Annette shooting the photo, and sure, that's me, and that's my striped shirt and raincoat, those things, and me, there in black and white, on that planning day, when I got measured and they did X rays and then even injected me with permanent tattoo dots that designate the treatment field; in the unimaginable event that I have to go through this again, the same area cannot be radiated, and the dots are the margins.

I think again, and find I'm not certain the photo was taken that same day. I've noticed that things in my head are out of the proper order—or missing—since all this began, since my situation has progressed from winter to spring to fall. I find this surprising because usually I remember every detail of every little thing, an ability that always has served me well in my interests and work, art and writing. It's a bit disconcerting not to have my usual form of recall. But maybe right now there is too much in my mind.

I've been dealt this, and am wading through without a map. Robert Lipsyte captured the situation perfectly in the title of his memoir *In the Country of Illness,* his own travels through cancer. This experience truly has been like going to a different part of the spinning globe. New surroundings, language, customs, food, form of dress. I look around the waiting room, around the hospital, around my immediate world. It seems nobody escapes life without, at some point, being sent to an unknown continent.

In the little corner of the world I always knew, two very bad things happened right around the time of my diagnosis. Nine days before it, in the next town over, less than half an hour after her mother dropped her at the town beach, a sixteen-year-old lifeguard disappeared from her post. Three months later, despite land and air searches and national exposure on *America's Most Wanted,* Molly Bish remains missing, and officials remain baffled. I once covered for my paper the school committee on which her mother serves, and she always stuck in my mind due to the biblical spelling of her first name: Magdalen. No one can guess the country where Molly now finds herself, just as they cannot imagine the one Magdalen now inhabits. Five days before my diagnosis, in my very same village, a guy who was a year ahead of me in high school died after years of struggling with illness. Tim Kargol had married Becky Dobek, a girl from my class. When they were first going out—our second year of high school—he took me aside and asked me what was the deal with how women's clothing was sized, because he wanted to buy Becky a shirt with his team number on it. What does she wear now, in the place where this loss has put her?

I see Tim's grave on my daily walk. I read the updates on the search for Molly. These losses are benchmarks for me. What was happening in my life back in the summer, what has happened to theirs. I've gotten out of the habit, but for them I fumble to find prayers, something in a language we can all understand, no matter where we are.

Annette is back at work. She says she doesn't feel 100 percent, but she's back, and I'm happy about that. She tells me she has a horse. She says it's a paint. I say I love paints. She says that it's not that pretty a paint. But what horse isn't pretty, I wonder? It's perfect horseback riding weather. She points that out and I agree. It is the end of September, but the temperature is more like summer than the actual season was, so it is a good time for anything. If you are in the mood.

I wait for my car at the valet hut. The hospital has a hotel flair in that way, a drive-up entrance with a wide, weather-beating overhang, and a staff of red-jacketed valets who, with varying degrees of sluggishness or speed, will park and retrieve your auto. This service comes in handy if you are very late, as I was today due to Big E traffic, so I stand in the line with my claim ticket. I allow a woman coming from obstetrics to go in front of me because she appears infuriated. She tells me she's been at the hospital since one o'clock, just for a single procedure: amniocentesis. It's now four. Three hours, she notes, in case I can't do simple math. I say it has to be a busy department, though I don't know this for sure, but baby places usually are, everybody having babies as they are these days. I wonder if I should add that I hoped the test went well for her—but what if it didn't? So I don't say anything. The valet drives up in the woman's car. It's an SUV thing with a shade in the back window to protect a child from sun, and a fancy jogging stroller folded in the trunk area. Unless she is incredibly prepared, this is obviously not her first time around with a baby. She gets in the vehicle and slams the door.

~~~

Back at home, I receive a greeting card. Addressed to me but sent to the wrong street, it finds me anyway. The woman who wrote it says she heard at the Ladies Guild that I am having a medical problem and she wants me to know she is saying some prayers for me. Whatever the reason, the word "some" sticks out for me. As if there are several she left out, or she only had time for a couple. She writes, "It's too long for you to remember (you were too young) but I had the same problem while I was cooking at school." She doesn't say what the problem was, but I guess it is clear. And, no, I didn't know that about her; I know that she used to cook at parochial school. She and another lady ran the kitchen and they used to blow up their rubber gloves like balloons before they put them on, to unstick them so they could fit their hands in and wash the dishes. They served Spam and shepherd's pie and, on Fridays, tuna fish and noodles. I can't think of one thing I liked to eat there. I was fussy about food and eventually got permission to carry my own lunch, which meant I had to sit in the corner with a diabetic who did the same thing except she had a good reason. Me, I was just a spoiled kid there at the end of the last window table with my thermos of Beef-aroni. The woman who used to cook the food that I didn't like to eat writes to me, "We take the 'ups and downs' as they come and pray for the best." She puts the "ups and downs" in quotes, just like that.

# ❧ 5 ❧

The walk from the hospital's main door to the radiation oncology department is a long one.

It begins at the entrance. There are women from obstetrics, in housecoats and looking tired and pale, headed into or out of the lobby for their post-delivery walks, pacing, dragging their IV poles into the fresh air, standing beneath the overhang arching their backs and squinting into the sun. There are fully dressed women leaving with their new babies packed in little carriers. Alongside them move women friends, men, grandparents, children carrying pastel flower arrangements or holding the strings to blue or pink metallic balloons shaped like pacifiers. There's a gift shop just inside the entrance to obstetrics and all it sells is baby gifts. Clothing and stuffed animals and blankets so you are saved if you arrive for a visit and haven't brought a present. At face value, this is a happy hospital entrance—expectation, fulfillment, the world renewed.

To get where I'm going, I pass the gift shop door and take a right off the lobby, the door after the easel that bears a sign warning you to stay out if you have the flu, which is odd, considering that this is a hospital. This leads me into the old wing, downhill from the main entrance. My lead-lined room is built deep into the hillside. I pass through a brick hallway featuring some kind of ceramic mural on the left wall. I don't know what it's about. I don't stop to study it. The theme seems to be people working together, and there are faces, multicultural ones, and there are names stamped into the clay. Maybe donors, I'm not sure. If you take a left after the mural, you will be headed to WOUND CARE and HYPERBARIC CHAMBER. Today, an elderly couple was standing at this junction and the woman was pointing down that hall and reading the sign loudly, like a tour guide. "That's where they have the hyperbaric chamber," she said. And he said, "The what?" And she said, "The hyperbaric chamber." He said, "Oh. Hyperbaric." I don't take that left. I turn right. I follow the sign: RADIATION ONCOL- OGY. I look at that sign when I pass beneath it, much the way I looked at the guy standing on the turnpike overpass the other day—it's hard to believe the sign is there and, same time, what does it mean? It's like the first few times I looked at my father's headstone. The words seemed from another alphabet. It was his name, but I was unable to read it. I didn't have the translation. These words on the panel hanging from the ceiling, they are meant for me. They tell me where I have to go, but I can't make sense of them. I just see lots of *o*'s and other rounded letters.

Every turn I take, there is another sign reminding me of the direction I'm going. Hitting me over the head with it. Over and over. You have this. You have this. Cancer. Cancer. You are going to the radiation oncology department. I was visiting this very hospital for a newspaper interview maybe twenty years ago and I saw the word "oncology" on a door I was passing. I think I'd just learned that meant the cancer department, and I remember thinking it would be horrible to have a reason to go through that door. I also remember feeling grateful simply to be walking past it, to be in the building for no other reason than to ask somebody my list of questions and be free to go back to the office and get a paper cup of Tab from the machine and sit down and write my sixteen inches. Now I follow that word. It sends me veering left, past some elevators that always have a steady flow of people waiting or leaving, lots of them with medical uniforms on. Carrying files. Wearing scrubs. Or fine suits. All of them looking important and, even if they're really the ones who wash down the floor after the heart bypass, looking capable of saving ten lives a day.

Then comes the room where you go if you need a birth certificate. And then the one that headquarters the hospital's couriers. There is a lot of activity here involving men in walking shorts. They all bear good calf muscles from running around the hospital and on errands around the city all day. Past them, I keep straight on, following the signs, then take another left. The hallway gets wider, less populated. More signs. There's a dead end. You now have two choices: HOUSEKEEPING, or RADIATION ONCOLOGY.

I don't have a choice. What I need is through the doors straight ahead. So I push one of them open and Angela, the receptionist, who seems to know the name of everybody within fifty miles, says brightly: "Good afternoon, Miss Shea."

OK, I do have a choice. I could have skipped all this. Since my diagnosis, a raft of people have floated forth with their suggestions for alternative—now called "complementary"—therapies. Take these vitamins, visualize that, don't eat those, go to this clinic. One says don't do anything at all, like her friend who willed away her cancer so many times she couldn't even count them. If all I had to do was think it away, it would be gone to the other side of the world. But I'm chicken. Full of the fear the guru spotted right off. So I went with the party line. I had the conventional surgery and now I'm having the conventional radiation. Therefore, here I will be, into the beginning of November. I can't say the actual date because I don't want to know for sure. I do know I'm to be coming here for about six weeks, but if I knew the exact number I think it would be a bit too overwhelming. So I keep that information from myself.

"Friday already," Annette announces when I climb onto the table with the help of the little metal stairway she carries over to the machine so you won't fall off and sue the hospital. "One week down."

# ❧ 6 ❧

You get weekends off.

You're supposed to relax and repair your body, which is working overtime to create more cells to replace what's been attacked. And your skin needs a break as well. In time, it will get burned worse than the skins of my sister and her gang who smeared themselves with Johnson's Baby Oil and fried on their sheets of tinfoil during our childhood summers at Hampton Beach. If you received too many treatments in a row, that would be detrimental inside and out. So radiation is like an office job. Monday through Friday. With Saturdays and Sundays as your own.

I no longer have an office job. Five years ago, after nearly fifteen years in journalism, I left the newspaper to concentrate on my fiction. A nice combination of having lots of people other than my relatives actually buy my books, and being on Tommy's health insurance, allowed me to live the fulltime writer's life, which I started the same month O.J. was beginning his criminal trial.

My routine is not complicated. Generally I wake when I wake, I walk, then I write until "The Young and the Restless" comes on TV. I lunch with them, then go back upstairs to write some more, and usually knock off in time for another walk and a pleasant night of whatever else is interesting me, alone or with Tommy along. He and I have never had a traditional nine-to-five-honey-I'm-home household. When we first were married, he covered the Red Sox. When they were at spring training or at Fenway or on the road, he was along with them. He worked nights to my days, and then days to my nights. When we did get on the same shift for a while, the unpredictability of our assignments and the availability of sources and subjects made for crazy hours. Shared time has been treasured, as has been the time we've each had to ourselves, heading to our polar-opposite favorite getaways—his including Manhattan and movie theaters, mine being anywhere that is outdoors and away from places like Manhattan.

So my first Saturday "off" from treatment, while Tommy sleeps, I head to the river in my kayak. I love this boat, which fits neatly on the roof of my old blue Honda and most summers is kept up there so I can visit the river whenever I like. When the moon is at its fullest, I'll paddle to a wide cove while owls call and beavers slap their unnecessary warnings and I'll float there in the light that you have to enjoy while it lasts.

But mornings aren't too shabby, either. There is mist after the cold night, and the new sun warming the air. Some of the moisture on the river forms shapes that I float right through. It's very much like being in the sky, clouds all around and beneath. There was only one other vehicle in the parking area this early morning, a black truck. The people who must have arrived in that are up ahead, in a canoe. They are standing, which is not a very safe thing to do in a canoe, but they are fishermen and they are casting fly rods and they stand to do that. From a distance they look as if they are walking on the water. The sight is a lot more impressive from afar. As I paddle closer, they look less like something from the Bible and more like sleepy young men in flannel shirts and baseball caps that promote cigarettes and beer. They have a little electric motor on their canoe, and it's quiet, makes a little muffled throat-clearing sound. They use it to move out of my way a bit, but they don't otherwise acknowledge me.

One, then another, then another—I see three great blue heron. It is always thrilling to spot them on the river, so large and wild and prehistoric, but then there is a sorry feeling because my approach always causes them to fly away with their powerful low swoops that look beautifully easy but have to be full of great effort when you are a creature that size. I move to a spot in the weeds and put down the paddle and watch a tree alive with dozens of chickadees all singing and darting. Their sound reminds me of winter, when everything is quiet except them, out there phoebe-ing. I eat a package of Rollos for my breakfast as I watch them. "Milk chocolate," says the paper wrapper covering the golden foil. I'm thinking of giving up dairy products because, according to a book I am reading, they are a major cause of cancer and they are killing people left and right. I'm reading a lot of books on such things as cancer and its causes and treatments, both traditional and the others that folks are urging me to try. I research my top three suspects: dairy foods—I've consumed huge amounts, starting with a childhood that literally floated in the whole milk I drank from a quart-sized glass; high-tension wires—there is a huge avenue of them behind the woods that are behind my house, and upon my moving in, I was warned by a seemingly psychic family member who literally sing-songed I was going to end up with cancer; and computers—I've spent two decades parked in front of them. I'm also starting to think about the pesticides used in my yard. We had fruit trees when I was growing up, and they had their regular applications of hand-pumped bug spray. I played beneath those trees, in those trees. One of them I considered "mine." It was in the second row, counting from the back woods, between a Golden Delicious and the vegetable garden. I petted it and spoke to it and it told me things back. I found comfort in the slingshot shape of its two lower branches, and made meals of the Macs that dropped from above. Eating without much more than first quickly brushing them on my pantleg. There's that poison. Then there's kids, or the lack of them. The fact that the only ones I've ever had were the kind that chase cats and stick their noses into the crotches of visitors. If you don't have children, your fertile years are one big uninterrupted estrogenfest. And the more estrogen in your system, the greater your chances for cancer.

All those things to consider. Then there's just plain rotten luck. Shit indeed does happen. I know that. At least I thought I did.

Why did I get this? I sought the answer in books, some of them gifts, others recommended titles I tracked down. A few I just happened across. The first time I went to a bookstore after my diagnosis, the label "Cancer" on the proper bookshelf was to me like the sign for the radiation department. What was I doing in front of this word, looking at these books? Often the answer was that I was getting frustrated, not knowing where to start. I felt I needed a medical degree to wade through each ten-pound, dry-looking textish title, written with such detail I could have used it to do my own surgery at home. And I felt offended by the pun-laden approach of more user-friendly softcovers like *The Complete Idiot's Guide to Living with Breast Cancer,* which, despite being written by a pair of survivors, ignores the terror many of its readers have to be feeling. The guide's first chapter title: "It Ain't Gold in Them Hills"; radiation goes under the heading "Getting Nuked"; prostheses under "Boob in a Box." The chapter "Facing Death" is illustrated by a cartoon of a woman staring into the eyes of a sickle-bearing Grim Reaper. At my town library, I stood at the computerized catalog to look up my crisis, typing in "radiation" and getting those twenty listings for Hiroshima and Chernobyl. Nothing on the type of radiation with which I was becoming more familiar. I decided to go with the keywords of breast cancer, and there indeed were books, but I found them stored on the very top shelf. It is just the luck of the draw of the Dewey decimal system, yet I was annoyed. This was the same as putting books for the legless up that high. My left arm was still sore from the surgery, I was wary of climbing the little ladder, afraid of falling and doing more harm. My friend Susan was with me, and she did the steps for me, then handed down titles. *So You Have . . . How to Cope with . . . Living with . . . All About . . .* All also similar in their cover art, usually some drawing or painting or soft-focus photo of a woman's chest, clothed or otherwise. Usually colored pink. At the checkout, a librarian greeted me warmly. Then glanced at the titles. Then back at me. Quickly.

This sunny Saturday morning on the river, I have no books with me. Just my car keys and paddles and life preserver and Rollos. I sit in my boat and eat the Rollos and think about giving up dairy in November, after the treatments are done. But for now, I need Rollos. I eat the last, then I put my hand in the water. It's cool and clear and you can see way to the bottom, which in this river ranges from several inches to unseeable depths. Right here it is about a foot, the bottom a soft muck across which some horror-show water insect crawls along, doing its Saturday morning errands. This river surfaces as a small stream. I visited its beginning just a couple of weeks earlier. And I wonder, where is the water I saw that day? How far did it get in the time since? I think that maybe it's beneath me now, holding up the boat.

# ❦ 7 ❦

I walk. Every morning. Whether or not I feel like it.

First, the clothing. I keep it at the foot of my bed and I grab at it in the fuzz of waking and dress beneath the covers. Sometimes I pull everything right over the pajamas. I make no excuses that it's getting too cold. In the same way that I don't feel as good about myself if I don't write each day, I need also to walk.

The dog sleeps as I slip from the house. Tommy sleeps, too. He is not one for early exercise. A night person, his walks often take place so long after sunset that he wears one of those reflecting crossing-guard vests so he won't get creamed by a car. I like to take care of my loop so early that later on in the day I have to stop and wonder if I've even done it. I start on pavement, the road in front of my house. I keep off the side of it, easy steps on the soft earth beneath a row of my neighbor's white pines. Then along a flattened stretch of tall grass, and back onto tar when the road turns right and heads to the cemetery. That is my walking place. Down the dirt road edging a field, take the right at the cemetery's garage where, in better weather, Mr. Kszepka has the doors open and talk-radio playing as he repairs and otherwise tends to the various mowers. His grandson is in there with him often. A preteen allowed to drive a truck around the graveyard's small network of roads. I once called out to him as he passed, "Hey, do you have a license for that?" And he looked at me in the disgusted way kids do when adults say something stupid. In this weather, though, there is no Mr. Kszepka, no grandson. Just the two garage doors closed, their windows edged with condensation from the frosty night. There is a thermometer at the small door of the office. I check this for the temperature that has been decreasing steadily with each morning. Today, twenty-eight.

Past the garage, I walk on the parts of the dirt road that do not yet bear prints of shoes or deer hooves or bird claws or dog paws. I like to make my own new tracks. That opportunity ends when the road turns into asphalt as I approach the back of the cemetery and the final row of stones. This morning, a guy is praying at one that bears the name of his wife, and the date of her death, and his name, but not yet his date. He walks to his car and backs out before I come up to him. I keep on until the little circle with the wooden cross in the center, a sort of religious rotary. I take a left there and walk down the runwaylike part of the road that leads to another circle, the site of a chapel that has yet to be built. For several years now, there has been nothing but sand and weeds from which a couple of tubes for electrical cables emerge, ingeniously topped off by plastic bottles cut in half so the rain doesn't run into the pipes. A ground-dwelling bird that I have yet to identify nests in this circle some summers. It is a type that fakes dragging its wing so as to distract you from the fact its nest is nearby. Whenever it's done this for me, I've acted like I fell for it.

I complete this circle twice. After the second time around, I enter the field. I head for the woods and I follow along their edge, my route now a tractor-wheel rut all grassy and with oak leaves collected in it. A few weeks ago I was waking earlier in the morning and I'd almost bump into deer at the margin of the forest. They'd turn and flash their bottle-brush-white tails and run off loping like carousel ponies. They were big and healthy and gorgeous and close and we'd scare one another, would be together in that. I usually spot squirrels, always see birds, and each morning, sometimes two or three times, flocks of geese make stitches in the subtle quilt of pale gray sky and clouds. I hear them before I see them. Ten or so, up to sixty at a time. I know the figures because, once having read that these birds mate for life, I always try to count them, and feel a relief if the number turns out to be even.

The field curves to the right, so I'm doing that as well now, continuing along the edge and down into a little gully, up again, and at this point I always turn for no reason except to go back to where I came from, to where I first met the forest, then along its farther edge, almost up to the house that once belonged to the farmer who willed all this land to the church. Whatever he grew—corn maybe—the church is now planting other things here. You could look at it that way, if you wanted to. You could also say it is a sad place to go walking, and that maybe I don't need to be around graves right now. You could look at it that way, if you wanted to. But this has been part of my walking route for the fourteen years I've lived down the road from the cemetery. So I've kept it up.

I make it to the edge of the farmer's house, then cut back to the circle that's waiting for its chapel. Once there, I walk in the opposite direction, counterclockwise, four times in all. This number means nothing special, I simply always circle four times each morning on my way back. Then I'm headed back down the runway part, taking a right along the last row of headstones, passing the garage and taking the left down the road for home. Some days I visit a few graves. In the darkest parts of this experience I went to make my pleas to those who loved me while on earth and now might have connections that could benefit me. I begged my father, and my mother's parents, and Rosemary. Her Cioci Annie, too, her aunt, the woman who called that morning to tell me Rosemary was gone. I don't beg actively now. It's been six months since the annual appointment that kicked all this health adventuring into gear, and I don't want to be a pest.

After this morning's walk, I go to help my future sister-in-law address her wedding invitations. It's Sunday and I think it's a nice thing for her to include me in this activity. In six weeks, Christine will marry Tommy's brother Johnny. Tommy is the eldest, Johnny is the baby. A photographer came to the house when Tommy was an infant and shot a series of photos of him that fold into a neat accordion of immigrant parental pride, black and white after black and white of a teeny little Tommy squinting into the camera while being propped up by a pair of adult hands shielded by a blanket. When Johnny was in first grade and was asked to bring in his baby picture for show-and-tell, he had no choice but to borrow one of his siblings' portraits—by the time he came along, seventh and last in line, there was little enthusiasm for shooting pictures of yet another kid. What could be fodder for a an inferiority complex is instead just another story in Johnny's arsenal of humor. He is one of the funniest people in the world, bearing the perfect mix of dead-on delivery and timing. I'm thrilled he's marrying Christine, who brings fantastic desserts to any family gathering and, even better than that, is one of those people you sink into about five seconds after meeting, they are just so familiar and comfortable and there is no need to be on guard or fake. I liked her from the first moment.

Christine's big bridal shower at a restaurant in Fairview was the week after my surgery. I wanted to go but wasn't feeling up to it. I figure this one thing, licking stamps, I can do. Tommy heads off to play baseball in his Sunday afternoon over-thirty league, something he quit the day after I was diagnosed but, needing routine and distraction, returned to in time. I get the directions to Christine's parents' house, where the work party is to be held, and drive to Springfield and take the required left at Skooter's, which is a bar that has materialized in the building where I bring my computer for applications of extra RAM. At Christine's parents' house, the invitations await in shrink-wrapped plastic, white paper, green ink with embossed purple gladioli lined up on the left. There are reply cards that ask if you want prime rib or chicken or scrod. Another stack informs you where the reception is to be held. And little squares of tissue, pink and white, to go between these cards for formality's sake.

Christine's order includes a booklet containing invitation etiquette. Information on the manner in which you should address your guests. "Courtesy titles," this was called in the newspaper's Associated Press stylebook—Mr., Mrs. and so on. In this little invitation book, widows get addressed by their husbands' names, which makes no sense to me—shouldn't these women now finally be given the chance to use their own names? Take note that you should never write "No children allowed" on the card—you should alert your guests verbally to this rule, and won't those be fun phone calls? Everything needs to be addressed and stamped and put in the envelope according to correct order, the most important thing being that when you pull out the contents, they are facing you. It's like piecework, stacking the invitation then the tissue then the directions then the reply envelope then the reply card and slipping that all in the envelope with the recipient's name on it and fitting all that into a bigger envelope on which you write the name and address and stick with a stamp that Christine's father went out special to get, which appropriately reads LOVE.

There are five people here doing this work in a cozy little addition to the house, sitting at a kitchen table. Christine, her mother, her father, her sister-in-law and me, concentrating on the lists made by the bride, and the groom, and the two sets of parents. Other than the usual how are you, and initial conversation and offers of tea, the room is quiet as we work away the hours. Nobody discusses how I am, and I find this a surprising relief. I'm with people, but the focus is on something other than me. It's nice, and I even eat the bread pudding that is our reward when we're done, and I really don't like bread pudding. But you find you want to eat something that is not your favorite when people are so good and kind as to just treat you like normal.

"I'll stop by, I'll come over—will you be home?" My family wants to know this. My friends want to know this. Normally I am happy to have time with people I care about. But now I have trouble with this. I have trouble feeling like a patient, like someone who needs to be visited, looked at, fussed over. My mother knocks at the door with a vat of vegetable soup, then proceeds into the kitchen to set it on the stove and wash the dishes that fill the sink, and what else can she do, clean, dust, what else? How many people the world over don't have even one person visiting them when they aren't well? "Did you bring my ice cream?" the crinkled up little woman in the wheelchair asked me when I opened the door at a nursing home one day years ago to interview its director. I'd never seen this woman in my life. I had to tell her no, I had no ice cream with me. She insisted she'd asked me to bring her chocolate. She's rolling down the hall, next to me, rowing herself along the linoleum with her curled-up slippered feet, admonishing me: "Well, will you remember next time? Chocolate!" That was twenty years ago. I wonder who ever came to see her, whether or not anybody filled her request. Twenty years later, I have an embarrassment of riches—ice cream in more than one flavor, flowers in all colors, friends at all levels of concern—and I often am not in the mood for the attention. I can be sullen. Or downright crabby. I can best tolerate the company of Tommy and Cindy, and, some days, only Cindy. When I apologize for the distance I'm keeping, Tommy says to me, "You can feel what you feel, or you can be a plaster saint." And I don't want to be a statue, to stand here with my arms outstretched and a smile on my face, looking as if none of this bothers me, calling up a perky manner for the benefit of others. I keep thinking of the TV patients, the afflicted whose movies of the week wrap so neatly the package of the fall from the mountain, or the eating disorder, or the unfortunate diagnosis, and the subsequent challenges and ultimate life success. Oh, there might be a few scenes where a bud-vased lunch tray is overturned or a well-meaning balloon-bearing relative is read the riot act. But all in all, the mental part of what a person might feel when the shit indeed happens, I have never seen addressed on my television screen. A smooth, anti-septic, fast, photogenic fight and recovery is what is delivered, and is what people expect. I do have to say, it's also what I would have ex-pected of myself as an adult—and maybe that is a big part of the prob-lem. How many times do you really think of how you'd be if you were off your feet, as they say? My general upbeat, faith-filled manner would have had me guessing that if I ever got whacked by life, I'd not only look good in my hospital bed, I'd genuinely feel good, too. And I'd try to make others feel positive as well, reassuring them that I'd be fine soon, quoting inspirational verses, setting records in learning how to talk or walk or whatever was my lost ability. "That's just how I am," I'd tell those who asked how I did it. "I never once got angry about be-ing sick, I never once asked why did this happen."

After she got bashed in the knee and lay crumpled there on the walkway just off the ice rink, crying WHY ME WHY ME, lots of peo-ple were making fun of Nancy Kerrigan. Now I know: you get bashed out of nowhere, that's what you wail.

❦

Because of the disconnection I feel to those in my closest orbit, Susan, with whom I used to take dog walks almost daily and who is one of the people who've been very patient as I've not wanted to do much of any-thing "normal," buys me a doormat reading GO AWAY, wraps it and leaves it on my porch and then, heeding the request, leaves before I spot her there. Some friends and family, even before seeing the mat, think I don't like them anymore because of my not keeping in touch, and they tell me as much. I tell them I don't know who—or what—I like anymore. Other people remind me that I should cheer up, adopt a pos-itive attitude. Which only succeeds in delivering the opposite.

A few friends I don't have to stay away from—they take care of that for me—coming near at the first news, but only to tell me that because my cancer was detected early there is really nothing to worry about. One woman informs me that what I have is not real. That what Cindy had was real. What *I* have shouldn't bother me, this woman says. Then there's another camp who can't seem to understand why I would be feeling low at this time. Haven't a clue. When I think about it, I realize these are the same folks who never really could understand whenever I felt happy, could never fathom why I might like her, love him, live here, go there, eat—or not eat—that. So, really, how can I expect those same people to "get" this—the bad I am going through—when the good in my life was a mystery to them as well. But still, you hope. You want someone to be on the same plane, to nod along with you, and you don't care if they're just doing that to be kind. Validation is all you want. That what you feel—what you fear, what you hope—is genuine and real for you. Whether or not it makes sense to anyone else.

But because I am normally some degree of social, all this separation I feel is as odd for me as it must be for the people I am putting off. I find kinship in a news clipping I've saved since the summer but ignored until now. In a *New York Times* essay, the writer Alice Hoffman's experience mirrored my seclusion as she told how her work helped her through breast cancer.

"I removed myself from everybody but my closest friends and family," she wrote. "I told almost no one about my illness and instead turned to what I had always found most healing."

She meant her stories. I think of that as I write this: words, sentences, daily entries, a process, a regular schedule of dumping it all out. That is helping me.

## ❦ 8 ❦

My general practitioner thinks I need a hobby.

I go to see him for the required update on how the country's number-one antidepressant is working. I tell him it isn't helping. I say I can't relax at all and he says I need other things to think about and he's off again on a romp of topics: Buddhism, Hinduism, Christianity, the liberal ways of the world. He's like this. Chatty. All over the map. I like him. An appointment is always an experience. Doctors fly planes for relaxation, he tells me. They love detail and challenge, so they fly. But then, he stops and points out, when they think about their work, they lose their concentration and they crash. "You want me to do that?" I ask. "No, but it's what doctors do," he says. "You? Maybe you could jump out of a plane—you wouldn't be thinking about your problems then." I tell him how afraid I am of heights. Oh. He searches for some other suggestion. He can't be faulted for not wanting to help.

Next stop is the hospital, and the start of week two. As I did last week, I drive myself. I want it that way. Tommy would like to take me into the city each day, sit there in the waiting room while I have my treatment, and then put me in the car and take me somewhere fun. And I have plenty of offers from nice friends and family who want to chauffeur, and do more than that. Some of them even want to drive out from Boston in order to help out, more than an hour away. My friend Robbie once volunteered for the American Cancer Society's "Ride to Recovery" program, and she and her then-tiny son Andy escorted an older woman to and from her treatments. She tells me she has the practice, and is just waiting for me to say the word. It's another embarrassment of riches to have these additional offers, and to turn them down. But it's just that I want to do the driving. It makes me feel normal. The treatments do not make me feel ill, so there really isn't a physical reason I can't do it. I think people are more used to hearing about cancer patients receiving chemotherapy, and how they are in need of rides to and from the hospital. I do not have to have chemotherapy because the margins of my tumor were clear—think of a piece of mold you find in the cheddar you were looking forward to eating, how you have to cut way around the little veins of gray-blue in order to have the rest of the block edible. You've cut around the margins, which is what the surgeon did for me, and now the radiation will clear up any stray cells. When I first hear that adjective, I think of the strays, I think of the Wild West, and of cowboys galloping off after a steer who parted from the herd. The galloping cowboys will not make me ill. In time they might make me tired, but I still am fine enough to drive. There is not a rule against that.

Early on in this, I signed a paper authorizing the treatments. In that document I promised not to conceive during this time, I guess to avoid the birth of radiated offspring. Another sheet advised me against using scented soap or lotions or any other skin products, many of which contain metals that would clash with the radiation process. I was given a booklet with a rather 1960s game plan for avoiding the treatment's side effects. I was advised to sleep a lot, eat whole foods, wear loose-fitting clothing, put aside the deodorant, stop shaving body hair and ban the bra.

In a nutshell, my favorite lemon-scented shower gel, along with careless sex, were on hold. But nobody said anything about driving.

On the way home from the hospital, I follow a sheriff's car. I count the heads inside. Two in the front seat. The smaller person in the back is slumped. I know where they're going because the road toward my town also is the road to the jail. Somebody is being delivered there. Somebody who looks young enough to be going from the end of his day at the grammar school to the start of his weekly Scout meeting. In bad times over the years, I've thrown myself onto a person who's passing by. Does this boy ever do this? Is he doing this with me right now, wishing he were someone else? I did that just today, when I observed the contentment of the grocery cashier, who, as she packed my purchases, said brightly to no one in particular, "I have Hamburger Helper at home. I made it before I came in today. Three Cheese. I put corn in it, too, to get the vegetables. It's waiting for me when I get home."

Though I know I'm wrong when I project that others have not a care in the world, for me, when I am feeling scared in the shadow of something I have no choice but to face, I'd just love to wake up as the woman who will spend her workday dreaming of the Three Cheese Hamburger Helper that awaits her.

## ❦ 9 ❧

The Walkman is here.

I admit I didn't think I'd be seeing this piece of electronics promised a week ago by my sister, who was to put it in the mail to me the very next day. She told me this in my kitchen, on the afternoon of my first treatment. I'd just come home, and I heard her voice downstairs. She lives out near Boston, an hour and a half away, so I thought I was imagining things. But no, Mary Ann was there, in my kitchen, on a late Monday afternoon.

Just as I am not a TV patient, we are not TV sisters. A three-and-a-half-year age difference seems to have been enough to put us long ago in different circles and different worlds. We no longer share a bedroom with an imaginary line dividing our respective halves (luckily for me, mine included the only door), but we continue to share a love of creativity. She's a painter and an art teacher and a pianist, and her talent has emerged again in her two lovely sons, the elder of whom is a skilled illustrator and budding bass guitarist and is there next to his mother when I go downstairs, and she greets me very loudly and enthusiastically with a big ten-thousand-watt, "How'd it go?!" She's smiling and all, but I can't help myself because this is not a smiley day for me so I use the same wattage to blurt, "I hate it!" Her face falls. She's tough, but right then I feel sorry for her and I apologize. I tell her about the machine and the room and the lousy music and somehow in an instant she's telling me she has a Walkman for me. She was going to send it. She will be sending it. Tomorrow. It will help pass the time at the hospital, she tells me. I agree it will.

I've been waiting and waiting, and no package for a week. She's busy, I figured she forgot her promise. This day, this Monday, the same day I went to the bank and got out the money to purchase one myself, the box arrived. Priority mail. From my sister. Nice little player, with a radio even, and comfortable headphones. I've never had a Walkman before. I've never had radiation before. A new era.

This afternoon, I show the Walkman to Annette. She tells me she loves music. All kinds. Including rock, and the Irish stuff her family always tuned in to weekend mornings. She recently heard a guy singing opera in Italian on an olive oil commercial and is trying to find out who he is so she can go and get a recording by him. She wants to know what I am listening to as she shifts me around and I don't help her. I hand her the headphones. I'd put in a tape I made myself a while back on the little boombox in my office. Tom Waits is scraping out "Hold On." I remember a *Rolling Stone* article years ago on Rickie Lee Jones, who had been holding a hospital vigil for a relative during the time she was dating Waits. He'd go to the stairwell and sing, an appropriate place for a voice like that, its bottom-of-the-barrelness resounding all the way down to the morgue in the basement. I'm in a hospital now and he's in my headphones telling Annette, "God bless your crooked little heart." She says she's not heard of this singer before, and isn't he unusual. I say yes, and that whatever you think of him it beats the radio, on which Gloria Estefan is urging me to come on shake your body baby do that conga.

≈≈≋

There are visitors at my in-laws'. People from Ireland, which is where Tommy's parents emigrated from as young adults, meeting for the first time in America after having grown up in tiny villages ten miles apart. My father-in-law has been here since 1949, but he never actually left Ireland. "Every day, Sean walks the fields of Cahir in his mind," his sister once told us, and she was, as they say there, dead on. His interests, his pals, his dreams both achieved and unfulfilled, all arc back to his place of origin. My mother-in-law also arrived here in 1949 but is one hundred percent American. Give her an early-bird special at a chain restaurant for dinner, a bus trip to Hampton Beach for the day, Regis Philbin making millionaires on TV and a Sunday paper full of coupon circulars to clip from, and the woman who first wore shoes when she was seven going on eight is in heaven. Both of them have always been great to me, but I especially love my mother-in-law, about whom not one of the traditional jokes applies. I always look forward to visiting, including on this day, a stop I decide to make after my treatment because I'm going to be passing the house anyway, there on its sloping hill above the hospital.

After I greet the visitors, everyone there at the table eating their chicken, and the potatoes that my father-in-law is finding inferior despite having inspected them himself before purchase, I'm taking off my coat in the other room and my mother-in-law follows me in and whispers, "We didn't tell them what's going on with you." What am I supposed to say? I don't care who knows, and I doubt that the news would wreck the vacation of people I've never before met. But I just say fine, whatever.

If I didn't respect my mother-in-law, and if I were in the frame of mind for it, I would not agree. I would give the information, as I do now, quite often, responding to a casual "How are you?" with "I have cancer."

Then comes the look. I might as well have rattled off all the major profanities and crude names for body parts. But I don't do this for reaction. I need to say it. I tell this to the guru and she again backs me up. She knows I say the word because it is the truth and if I say the word the whole thing becomes more real for me. I have calendar pages

marked with doctors' appointments. A fat folder of medical information and bills and consent forms. A two-inch crescent-shaped scar on
the upper left quadrant of my left breast, and a one-inch railroad-
trackish double line of another just below my armpit. I go to the hospital daily to get radiated. I also have a very good prognosis. Yet, three
months after diagnosis, there remains an unbelievable quality to all
this. So saying the word is reality for me. This day, though, when asked
by somebody I care for not to mention it, I just say fine, whatever.

# ❦ 10 ❧

I'm to see the nurse so she can ask me how I'm doing and what's happening and all. She's standing in for the radiation oncologist, who left for vacation in Italy just after our first appointment. And I think that's how life is: you, Mary Ann—you over there—you get to go to Italy; and you, you go to the lead-lined room. I've been on the flipside of this, going places, Italy once, even, where Tommy and I stood with about a million people at the Vatican on a Wednesday afternoon and saw a little tiny white figure that was the far far away pope make his appearance in a window. An hour later, we're waiting in the Limbolike line for our allotted twenty minutes in the Sistine Chapel, which the guide is pronouncing "Sixteen" Chapel, and a man in front of us drops dead. Though shaken, we joined the rest of the world that did not know this man and we went on with our day. We finally made it into the chapel and watched conservators on scaffolding high above painstakingly removing centuries of grime from the masterpieces I previously knew only from color plates in my art history books. We sat at a nearby restaurant where the doors were open to the stunning day outside and we spent hours over baskets of bread and boatloads of olives. We walked in the midafternoon sun outside the Vatican walls, passing a tiny sedan in which a man and a woman unabashedly made love. We bought ices and a *USA Today* international edition and I cooled my feet in a fountain while Tommy caught up on the box scores.

When my first book was published, I was invited to appear on the *Today* show. Tommy and I were put up the night before in a snazzy Park Avenue hotel suite and were transported the two blocks over to the show by limousine. Turning the corner on this auspicious morning, we had to pause for rerouted traffic; to our right was a yellow city cab; on the pavement just in front of that, a still body covered with somebody's overcoat.

It's your normal day, or you are in Italy, or you're going on national TV. For someone else that same day is their last. Musical chairs. A game I never thought was fun.

~~~

The nurse who also did not go to Italy on this day asks me how many treatments I have left, and I tell her I don't know because I'm not counting. She has brought into the room a file on me the size of a photo album, and she flips it open. I can read my name and diagnosis. I don't like seeing that in writing. It's one thing to see it in your head, another to see the fact in print. And it's on the top of all the pages, like this is a phone book and me and my tubular carcinoma are the relevant city. The nurse flips, flips, finds what she's seeking: "Oh, you've had eight— how many left?" I tell her I don't know and I don't want to know. She offers: "Would you like me to calculate for you?" I repeat, no, that I don't want to know. "Some people want to know everything, every detail," the nurse responds. She doesn't know she's talking to somebody who wanted to be anesthetized for the operation a day before it was to be performed. "I don't want to know," I say. "Don't tell me." It's just too much right now. I know the number is in the double digits, and that it is high. I don't want to know more than that. "Some people want to know everything," the nurse says again, but this time she closes the file.

~~~

In the waiting room, I wear the Walkman and feel cool. It fits perfectly into the pocket of my radiation uniform, which amounts to a hospital johnny in white with various geometric designs and a navy blue zip-front hooded sweatshirt with pockets into which I've stuffed a collection of good-luck charms: a tiny Santa-shaped gift card bearing my grandmother's signature, a little red straw angel that was given to me on the day I was marked up for radiation, and a tiny picture of Rosemary and me, skin summer-pink as we're goofing in a Hampton Beach photo booth back in the summer of '76. The pocket also accommodates the Walkman, which today I've loaded with a new tape Tommy put together for me, leading off with a world-weary Bob Dylan saying plain as day that he used to care but things have changed. He never sounded better to me than right now as I'm sandwiched between the earpieces. I've never heard music through headphones and the detail and intimacy fascinates me. I'm staring at the usual spot on the floor, and there go the ballet shoes of the woman I couldn't look at the first day. I've spotted her a couple of times since, one day even nodded along while she and another patient compared notes on their antidepressants. This woman was saying how they were making her ill. The woman next to her said hers were doing the same thing, but then the doctor lowered the dosage. Yet another woman, seated across the way, chimed in how the first woman needs to do that, needs to ask for the decrease—why suffer, the pills are supposed to make you feel better, not worse. That is her point, and she says it. I'm thinking of my own ride on the country's number-one antidepressant, but I keep quiet. It's like a support group going, all of them on antidepressants despite all of them probably having read the same literature I did, the American Cancer Society booklet that everyone who lands here is given, the one that offers two sentences to the question "How Will I Feel Emotionally?"

"Many patients feel tired due to the radiation therapy, which can affect your emotions. You also might feel depressed, afraid, angry, frustrated, alone, or helpless."

Might? The antidepressant roundtable had heated up in less than a minute. Women who'd otherwise be separated by neighborhood, occupation, economics, race, sitting there in identical johnnies, acknowledging the identical need for happy pills in this place and time. I'd say the feelings of depression, fear, anger, frustration, loneliness and powerlessness should be emblazoned on the side of the radiation machine, much like the warning label on a cigarette pack. "If you do this, you're probably going to feel all these."

≈≈

This day I ask the woman in the ballet slippers—she has a name, Luz, that I overhear—how she is.

"Well, I'm not crying all the time like I was," she answers. "I used to get up in the middle of the night and cry. Now I just get up in the middle of the night and say, 'I have cancer.'" She tells me this in her accent and it comes out: "I hov consayer." And I start thinking how the word for the disease must exist in some form in all languages, and people all over the world, women all over the world, are getting up in the middle of the night, and crying or not, we're all just sitting there in the dark using whatever words we know, saying, "I have cancer."

I ask Luz her age. She's fifty, looks thirty-five and I remark on that and she tells me that's what everybody says. That she looks thirty-five, and that she has cancer.

# ⚓ 11 ⚓

This is how I get to the hospital:

Back the car from the garage and shut the door with the remote control that is in need of a new battery, working pretty well on "down," not always responding on "up." Then I put in a tape. I might go through the entire thing—one side equals one way on this trip, roughly thirty minutes. Or I might fall upon a song that holds some sort of word or two or three that I need to hear over and over, so I might repeat the tune the entire way. For instance, the trip takes roughly eleven listens of John Hiatt's "Before I Go," or Taj Mahal's "Freedom Ride." I know this from experience. Replaying a single song would be much easier with a CD player, just hit the button for the selection. But I don't have one of those in my car, which is ten years old and predates that technology. I do have a cassette player with a rewind button, and that's what I use to locate the beginning of the song once again.

All this and I'm not even at the bottom of the driveway, where I take a left and try not to look at the sad gap of air left by the guy across the street when he cut down the tree that to me always looked the shape of a strong flame. Especially in the fall, yellow-orange leaves burning there in beauty, now nothing more than a pile of logs that a man in a pickup will eventually come along to split and take away. I pass through the old railroad abutments, up toward the farm where the pumpkins are half price even though Halloween is still weeks away, over the little concrete bridge and through the beautiful flat watershed fields where as a kid I once went to a circus with real elephants and a freak-show wagon. Now up to Four Corners. Lanky baggy-jeaned kids are just out of high school for the day and they are all over the place, walking slowly and too far into the road solely because they can. Take a right at these lights, past the church where I was baptized and the school I attended for eight years that is now the parish center where you can play bingo on Thursday nights, onto the wider part of Main Street, past the French cemetery, then the French church and its sign telling of an upcoming craft fair. Next is the street of Alice, my honorary grandmother and my mother's oldest friend, the woman who taught her to make donuts on a series of long-ago Tuesday nights and whose late husband Freddie made great frog noises and took me to Mystic on my first deep-sea fishing trip, when I caught two small fish on the same hook at the same time.

Just after Alice's street is the funeral home patronized by the town's Polish people, conveniently just across from the flower shop and its owner, who said "shit" to me in my driveway when she delivered a floral arrangement and asked me what the occasion was and I told her what I had. "Shit," she said with honesty I appreciated, and to look at her, all neverfailing sweetness, you wouldn't think she would know how to line up the letters for that word. Past St. Stanislaus Hall, where the clerk recently faked a holdup and told the cops his register had been robbed at gunpoint, $1,200 gone, taken by a man in a mask, but he later recanted and admitted he'd simply helped himself. Drive down the dip to the main part of Main Street—the pub, pizza place, hair place, hardware store, dress shop, dentist, barber, bank, package store, milk store—and over the bridge where my sister once fell off her bike and cracked her head on the rounded metal railing and bled all over her avocado green vinyl coat that I no longer wished was mine. Someone recently has been seeing to it that American flags fly twenty-four hours a day along the bridge, even though it is not a holiday time. There is Tenczar's grocery and Chudy's hardware across from each other, then, across from the common, old Tambrands—once known as Tampax and once employer of several generations, and once a family threat ("Study or you'll end up working at Tampax"), now a "technology center." More children, the fire station, row houses, the river flowing on the right behind the blueberry farm, across the road from what used to be Hemlock Hill, where I spent childhood winter nights rope-towing to the top and skiing to the bottom, and Cindy, who did not ski, would go into her bathroom at a designated time of night and flick the light on and off and when I got to the top of the hill I could see the light blinking there from the patio-pink ranch up on the cliff across the river, a little bathroom beacon in the dark, my friend signaling me that she was out there.

Past the hill there is the skating pond on the left and then one on the right where I caught suckers with my father one Sunday afternoon ages ago, my hair in foam curlers because I had a church procession later in the day. The old soda plant on the left, then the house with the yard sign that welcomes you to the village and reminds you that my childhood neighbor, the polka park, is located here and open every summer Sunday. There's an odd stretch now, woods but also new houses—lots of new houses where there used to be nothing but forest and farmland. They are constructing another one in the pasture on the left where somebody used to graze a graceful palomino. Then comes Red Bridge, its little power plant and big dam that I always have found scary to pass by at night. Down the hill to another small bridge next to trees growing on tenuous little river islands, Leo's Glassworks, up a hill, the house I once thought I'd like to live in, a white farmy thing with an assortment of little barns and coops in the back, now neglected and tipping-over, structures I envisioned would have been perfect for chickens or goats. Now comes the house with just rocks for a front yard, and the turnoff for Poole Street, which my sister and I used to call the Corn Road because corn was most of what lined it back then, when we used to accompany my mother on her drive to pick up my father when he worked overtime at Uniroyal. On the way back, in a time of life when taking a different road home was a thrill, we begged her to return us home via the Corn Road please, and she would.

More big houses now, a little stand where you can buy honey, a deer-checking station with its scale and noose, the hearing-aid business, the general store, the turnpike overpass, the hill toward Ludlow Center. A right at the lights here on the crowded corner where the apartment complex ten yards off the busy intersection is named Country Meadows. People in Spandex and Polarfleece are speed-walking off the day. The school speed limit is flashing 20 m.p.h. but nobody is paying any mind. The crossing guard is pulling on an orange vest imprinted with his title. Right here, a few springs back, in all this area of commotion and heavy settlement, I once saw an enormous moose cross the road.

If I'm in a hurry, I now take the pike. But normally, I save the forty-five-cent toll and the speeding current of vehicles and drive farther into a residential section. I must first wait at another set of lights. Traffic is rolling through, a truck carting a load of trash, a printing company van, a sportscar, an empty bus. Green light. It's my turn and I go on to pass the condos with the tennis court, then the Portuguese cemetery that always shows some measure of activity and many flowers, most of them fake arrangements but very fancy and kept up. At night here, you can see fiery dots of twenty-four-hour votives burning diligently, blinking in the dark like animal eyes. At this point, the road is thick with houses. Then a four-way stop that always makes me think of the John Prine song set at such an intersection. Now, the home of an artist who decorates elaborately for Christmas with dioramas even inside her freezer, and each December holds an open house so anybody can go and look. A little grocery turned day-spa. Solar panels on a ranch-house roof. A pond that is home to swans. More lights, these at the turnoff for the jail. Then a place called the Liquorshed (I always think Liquors-head). Into Chicopee now, the childhood home of my father.

The entrance for a golf course, the headquarters of the refuse company that hauls my trash away. A convenience store with a sign that asks you WHY COOK GRINDERS 2/$5. An unremarkable cape that, in season, has a yard exploding with gorgeous perennials and you can go there and purchase some if you like, which for years I've wanted to, but have yet to.

State park entrance on the right. A firehouse. Now a deli, and a chiropractic office. Dragon House restaurant and Chicopee Savings. Subway, McDonald's, Motel 6, big two-story-tall statue of a white man marking the site of the embarrassingly named Plantation Inn. Straight onto the interstate now, you are just fed to it and then you're headed over the river where my father spent his boyhood walking and fishing and hunting and imagining. Past the exit for my pal Margaret, from my old reporter job, who is home on disability with a bad disk in her neck, and if that isn't enough trouble, is on the verge of getting a divorce. She is after me to visit her on my trips into the city, and I will, but not today. No time on this day so I go straight toward the hospital, passing the Smith and Wesson factory on the left, Jahn Foundry on the right, then Titeflex, a.k.a. The World's Leading Producer of Teflon Hose. The sign WELCOME TO SPRINGFIELD, Bee-Line Trailer Sales, Armory Street exit. Bear left for 91 North. Pass the Holiday Inn that used to have a revolving restaurant at its top and that still has a restaurant but not one that moves. Main Street-Chicopee-North Springfield: this is Exit 10. As you take this, there is a small blue sign to your right—BAYSTATE TRAUMA CENTER. The word "trauma" is outlined by a white box, maybe to make it stand out. Go down the ramp to the stop sign. Cross Main. Go up the little street. The hospital will be right in front of you.

There's a stoplight here. Take the right, then the quick left for Wesson and North Campus. The valet in shorts, standing at the next stop sign, will want to take my car and park it. Unless I am in a hurry, I say I'll find my own parking spot. Thanks, don't help me.

# ❦ 12 ❦

I am late today. It is the Friday that begins Columbus Day weekend. I see this on my calendar. I also see the date squares I've colored in with yellow highlighter to remind myself I have some book promotion event scheduled. I'll put that in the past tense. I had them scheduled, and then I canceled them. "For health reasons," I told some of the contacts, who usually responded they hoped it wasn't something serious, and I'd say "thanks," or "cancer," depending on my state of mind.

I usually do about a hundred readings, talks, signings and interviews in a year to help my books find their way into the hands of readers. If you aren't a writer who falls into the household word category, and you want to keep doing this sort of thing for a living, you must do what you can to get the word out. I've appeared on Tom Snyder's midnight TV show, and also at my parish picnic. Was interviewed in Washington, D.C., on Voice of America radio, which can be picked up around the globe, and played my accordion on Mitch Moskal's "Early Bird Polka Show," a favorite of area farmers when it beams out from UMass at Amherst's WMUA-FM every Saturday morning at 5:30. As it was with newspaper work, with this new job, no two days are alike. The eight things I was to have done this month—three libraries, two book groups, one women's business club, a bookstore and a reading to benefit the local food pantry—were postponed or canceled, as I hadn't the energy or interest. My book-related work is now limited to things I can do at home—the writing of a new novel, and the editing of the one I've just finished. The publication dates are next summer, and then the spring after that. I cannot imagine completing either of the projects, nor can I envision once again being out in the world enough to do the necessary promotion. Suddenly, fiction in general is seeming trite to me and I wonder how I will ever complete the new story. Things that are made up, artificial, put on, bother me more than ever, and the fiction I always saw as "real" because it contained honest emotion no longer seems so. I'm also getting sick of extra stuff—possessions seen as necessities that I now realize I really don't need. I find myself giving away, tossing out, donating, and it has helped calm whatever is rearing up in me right now.

I can't do anything about the mess of cars on the roads today. Despite the rain, everybody is out to see the foliage. They don't care about the rain. They just want to have a holiday weekend.

The trees are well into turning. I drive down corridors of orange and red and brown. I'm noticing this, but I'm not enjoying the post-card scenery in the way I normally would, with walks just to admire and the camera out and ready and finding a few leaves to take home and press in a book and forget about until maybe years later when I open the book again and there they are, flat and fragile and perfect. My favorite trees are those that wear a blend of colors, usually with some salmon thrown in. Today I've yet to spot one of this type.

I stop again at my in-laws, who are just back from taking their visitors on a bus trip to Vermont to see what New England is really supposed to look like. One stop was a cemetery containing monuments carved from the state's famous granite. A tour guide got on the bus as it entered the cemetery, and pointed out the most unusual ones. My mother-in-law tells me there is a stone carved in the shape of a bed containing a man and a woman holding hands. According to the guide, the man loved the woman so much that after her death he wore her clothes to work. I ask what type of a job did he have. Turns out the guide hadn't said. My mother-in-law notes that there was a small stone at the foot of the bed, to mark the resting place of the guy's second wife. I guess he wasn't that broken up after all.

And I think how I wouldn't want anybody too broken up over me. This is one of the things cancer makes you do—think things like that, stay awake, fret, take a piece of green construction paper on the night before your surgery and outline what you want done with your body, and your funeral plans, down to the food and music at the after-party, and a list of who you'd like to come by the house for their pick of your possessions. You watch your hand writing the word "cremation," because you never did find out how to be donated to science; you write your request for vegan cuisine and to play the Saw Doctors and Padraig and the old country accordion stuff by Gary Sredzienski. "Tell everybody to enjoy," you write. "And tell them to go on and make good use of their time." You add that in, even though you don't feel you are practicing that yourself right now. On a good day, though, wasting time is a pet peeve. So these will be your words from beyond, written now, on this green construction paper and put in an envelope that you don't know how to label. Even if you have every reason to be hopeful, this is what the name of this disease is scary enough to do.

≈≈

In the radiation oncology locker room, there are three cubicles. Inside each, there are three hooks and one bench. You change here into the hospital johnny you've taken from a cabinet. On my first day, I was told not to leave valuables in here. But I see that enough people do, handbags hanging, keys visible. I wonder who would steal from such a place, but I guess that anything is possible. Today, I enter the cubicle way on the right and there on the bench is a sweater with a wig on top of it. It's short and white, as if somebody shed half her head there. Or maybe, for the wearer, it's nothing more than leaving a headcovering behind. You see the women enter the department and they come through the door and sweep off their wigs just like that. Like hats unnecessary in a warm place. So the wig should be no big deal to me. Even so, I change quickly to get away from it, this reminder of how serious all this stuff down here is, what some people are made to go through, what I did not have to face. Wig people are chemotherapy people. I remember how awful Cindy felt during those treatments, and in the eight years that have passed, I have had some idea of how often she has wondered about the lasting effects of the drugs she was given, just what might be the fallout.

I watch Annette call for and escort down the hall a man who is a new patient with a tricky name. She asks for a pronunciation. The man is cranky. She cajoles. Asks about his day. They disappear around the corner.

"You enjoy your work?" I ask this as Annette adjusts the machine when it's my turn, making the red line hit its mark on the center tattoo. The ink and tape covering the tattoo are beginning to come off. She draws me some new lines, teal blue this time rather than the original purple, and she tells me she loves this job. There are always nice people, each and every day, she says. I ask, isn't it depressing seeing these people, day in and day out? And how about dangerous?

"People have the wrong idea of what we do in here," she says. "It's not Chernobyl."

Then she leaves the room and the door closes and the flashing light on the ceiling starts its whirling, warning everyone not to enter the room in which I've been left.

# ❦ 13 ❦

A saint and some songs arrive in today's mail.

The saint is a rerun, another Peregrine. But I'll take him. I like saints. Most have pretty good stories attached to them, and they were, after all, actual real people to start off with. In another place and time, they were the nice guy next door. The crabby woman down the road. The kid you tipped a drachma for delivering your morning paper. I'm not sure where or when Peregrine lived, but like most saints, before he got the power to heal or levitate or have visions or whatever was his saintly ability, he started out like you or me, probably was somebody's favorite uncle, maybe was always late for holiday dinner, didn't like peas, had a succession of dogs all with the same name, could dance surprisingly well when the opportunity came along.

The version I get of him today, while very fancy and complete with its own attached holy medal, reveals no such facts about his private life. This painting of him, clearer than the card I already have, shows Peregrine standing in front of a house or some similar type of building. He's got a cool-looking long cape on—a maxi-length we used to call it—and a little black hat. He's holding a cross and a cane. A pouch hangs from his belt. He's got the cape opened a bit so you can see his leg, which is bleeding all over the place. The other Peregrine I got sent had just a little wrapping on his ankle, hardly larger than a Band-Aid. This one is in bad shape. On the back of the card is his prayer. Peregrine is, I learn from this, 'The Patron Saint of Serious Diseases.' Not just your ordinary ones, this implies. Don't go bothering him with a cough or itch. He's here for the biggies. When you need to call in the troops.

The card informs me that Peregrine had cancer and that he knows how to intercede. His picture is engraved on the front of the medal. On the back are the words PRAY FOR US ITALY.

So all of Italy has been asked to pray. For us. For us all. 'PRAY FOR MOLLY' read the buttons that are circulating now. They bear a picture of the smiling teen, and that request below. Over the weekend, three hundred kids were photographed and fingerprinted at a Molly-inspired safety-identification event held in an area candy store. Molly's sister, Heather, brought her fourteen-month-old daughter, who was the first in front of the digital camera, the first to have her tiny fingers rolled in ink. "It's sad that you have to prepare for something like that," Heather said in the newspaper story about the event, an article that also noted Magdalen was there wearing another button, one that read nothing more than the word HOPE. I hear that word a lot these days. People are hoping things. They are hoping I am feeling better, they are hoping they will see me soon, they are hoping for the best. It's a nice word, I see it as a candle flame. Put enough of these together and the light is strong enough to get you through the forest.

The flame I receive today is in a padded envelope stamped with a foreign postmark. Air-mailed from Ireland. A tape for the Walkman, from Padraig, who not only put the songs onto a cassette but wrote them himself. Songwriting is his art and his work, and he's given me a gift of it. The cassette is decorated with tiny stickers. A star, a heart, a little red Corvette, a black electric guitar, a cup of tea. And a long white one on which he's printed the tape's title: *Songs for a Lead-Lined Room.*

In the note attached, Padraig offers his own hopes, that the music will be distracting when I'm in the hospital and focusing when I'm in the car. I am in that car when I first listen to it, parked in the lot next to the little post office where I rent a box. As I watch the Saturday errand-goers hustling in and out of the building, I receive the sweetness, his thoughts of me in better times and terms, telling me my spirit never falters. The faraway-held confidence makes me shift in my seat—I'm thinking he should see me nowadays, faltering left and right.

But there in the old blue Honda, the music cuts through my self-doubt and plows it aside gracefully as a prow of a boat moving through dark water. I lean easily into the song about the wide sky and the ocean in a place I've never been. I'm there nonetheless. People parked on both sides of me are checking the bottom line on bills and tossing unwanted flyers onto their car floors, exchanging gossip through rolled-down windows. Between them, I'm a world away, beneath the wide sky, watching the surf tumble smooth oval rocks and spirit them, with wave language, onto the beach where I stand.

# ❦ 14 ❧

It is now October.

Breast Cancer Awareness Month.

I am extremely aware of breast cancer right now. Even if I weren't, there's a good chance I'd get the idea. The TV features a series on it, the radio broadcasts its lists of classes, the papers run stories, people are calling me to put the television on now, or switch on the radio, or here's a clipping I saved for you.

Somebody gives me a copy of *Self* magazine. It has the lead headline of "Surprise! Thin Thighs. A Quickie Plan for Very Sexy Legs." I look down at my legs, not my concern right now. But neither are they the reason I've been given this magazine. Up in the corner of the front page, just to the right of Cindy Crawford's mole, is an alert boasting *Self*'s tenth annual Breast Cancer Handbook. I am invited to "Tear it out. Protect yourself." Too late, but I flip to the section anyhow.

❧❧

Octobers past, I was one of those people clipping the stories and passing them along, in this case to Cindy who, being what some term a survivor, certainly would want to read them, right? I saved for her, alerted her, all along the way of the eight years since she was diagnosed and had the mastectomy and the chemotherapy and went on to the great effort of resuming life in the wake of all that. I felt I was doing her some good.

But then I landed on the receiving end of all this. And I realized that, no matter how well-intentioned the piece, most of what was being put out there for Breast Cancer Awareness Month was devoid of information or simply was feel-good material that skirted reality. The *Self* issue ran its share of stories about testing and diagnosing and treatments, but most pages were peppered with stylized boxes all bearing the same "What I did on my summer vacation" lead-in:

"I had breast cancer and now . . ."

The dot-dot-dots were followed by accomplishments including adopting a child, starting up an outdoor-adventure company, learning to speak French and noticing the grass growing. All good and admirable stuff, but I found it horribly off-putting. I searched the pages for the boxes that began with, "I had breast cancer and then I fell off the edge of the earth and was hanging on by, like, one hand, then four fingers, then three, then two, then one, having tons of people who wanted to help but still feeling that alone, that freaked out, that misunderstood, and then I had surgery and treatments and needed to think for a thousand days, but now . . ." Then—only then—could come the new career as a gluten-free restaurant chef or the life as a foster parent for at-risk teens from a dozen third-world countries. Let's have some acknowledgment of the middle part of the process. Please.

Everyone's experience is not the same, certainly, but I spotted a canyon of a void in most of the recountings. One forty-four-year-old survivor wrote that because of the magazine's annual awareness efforts, she had been diagnosed early. "I never felt my life was in jeopardy," she stated in the intro to the special section. "I always say I had 'breast cancer lite.' " This made me crazy. Would readers who'd never been anywhere near this experience think, oh, fine, cancer can be really nothing. What's the big deal about this disease, anyhow? I guess I really don't have to go for one of those gawd-awful mammograms. And, hey, if I do get cancer, it sounds like I maybe get to finally open that craft shop! I wanted some writer, or reader, to mention the hopeless feelings. How the disease messes with not only your body but your mind and life and those who populate it. How the whole prospect of cancer being such a huge killer swings the klieg light onto every problem you ever had, including those you were aware of and those you thought you'd sufficiently dealt with and put to rest years before; I found none of that in these stories. Instead, everything, all of it, sunny.

Sunday's *New York Times Magazine* runs a section in honor of the month. The pages are mostly ads for the new wave of drugs that maybe-might-could, just perhaps but we're not totally promising, reduce your chances of breast cancer or its recurrence. The editorial content is limited to brief simplistic stories on self-detection and treatment. There is one on radiation, and my eyes fly to that. The title is an imaginative "Radiation." Below is a large photo of a woman racing along on a bicycle, moving ahead with such speed that the background is nothing but a blur. From this illustration, you might think that to undergo radiation you must put on a tight little racing suit and get on a bicycle and pedal as fast as humanly possible. I wish it did. Physical stuff I can handle. Putting one foot in front of the other, as I do on my walk each morning, that is easy to me. It's an easy, unthinking accomplishment. You get from there to here. You're done. Mental stuff is a lot tougher. This month, or any other.

# ❦ 15 ❧

On the walk, as I have for years, I find a piece of trash somewhere along the way and bring it home to my bin. I feel it's the least I can do for the earth in exchange for the pleasure of moving along on it. Once in a while I bring a bag along and collect more than a few pieces, though I have not done that this year. Right now it is all I can do to follow my route and then at some point select the Wendy's cup or the Burger King wrapper or flattened Bud can. I prefer handling trash that is recognizable—a couple of years back I had a nasty experience when I unknowingly lugged home a roadside bag of vomit. Today I picked up what I thought was cardboard. Two pieces. Turned out to be a flattened book. *Ghost Liners* by Robert D. Ballard, who is described there as "Discoverer of the *Titanic*." I didn't bring home all the pages because some of them must have come off when the book got run over, but there are enough to enjoy if you want to take the time to flip through, which I did, in my continuing search for the meaning of the people and experiences and *Titanic*s placed in my path.

The first illustration was a big color photograph of the *Titanic* wreck. The telemotor control that once held the ship's wheel. A section of bow railing. There were photographs of some of the victims as they looked in life before this tragedy, and some showing them after they were saved. And one of a porcelain head, which was all that remained of an expensive French doll. Robert D. Ballard theorized it might have belonged to Loraine Allison of Montreal, the only child from first class who did not survive.

There are more doomed ships as you get farther into the book, including the *Empress of Ireland,* which went down in the St. Lawrence River two years after the *Titanic* sank. There are photos of its wreck. Its stairs, a lifeboat still fastened on deck, a lonely human skull amidst the wreckage. Additional sad stuff is found in stories of the *Lusitania,* the *Stockholm,* the *Andria Doria.* There is the *Britannic, Titanic's* younger sister, built to be even more dazzling than the firstborn. Ballard writes that she was "an innocent victim." A hospital ship painted white, with big red this-is-a-hospital-ship crosses on the hull that did not matter to the German submarines in 1916. Which is how life can sometimes be.

Some tiny submarines have shot at me, and have hit their mark. I didn't feel it at the time, but the damage was done and here I am feeling very bottom-of-the-ocean. My family and friends are floating by in their little contained diving bubbles. I see their faces at the windows, looking at my wreckage. They are saying, ah you're fine. You'll be great. Think positive. Be happy. Have a cup of tea. It could be worse, they say, you hear about people who are in their twenties with two kids and they get cancer. I'm forty-one with no kids. Older, and with just Tommy, fewer people to worry about me, or, ultimately, miss me, so that makes it better, I guess.

Luz—who is fifty and who looks thirty-five and who has cancer, with three kids and one grandchild, all of whom live with her—is in danger of losing her job because of having to be at the hospital each day for her radiation. She tells me all this in the waiting room, where she is crying. It could be worse, and here it is in front of me in 3-D full-color Kleenex-plucking real life. Luz says she is too tired to go back to her office after coming here. She just can't do it. Just can't. She sleeps every possible moment, when she's not up in the middle of the night saying,

"I have cancer." The staff here is supposed to help her explain all this to her boss, to get her the correct paperwork, including a nicely worded reminder that it is against federal law to discriminate against cancer patients.

"I can't do it much longer," Luz tells me, and she is looking right at me then and I am looking right back. "You know?"

I don't know, and that is the thing. Tommy is self-sufficient and supportive. The dog requires only two quick feedings a day, and a few trips in and out of the house. I'm on my own schedule at home, long ago having shed any connections to what could be considered a boss hanging over my head and threatening my financial future. But I nod to Luz that I know, because, by now, the start of my third week of this, I know what to say to somebody else in here—most often, the truth, however it sounds. But this time a lie would be better, I think. So I tell her, "I know."

I go home. I do the work that I do. I write this, which slowly is becoming the total of all the words I put down each day. Other than that, I do my walk, I knock around the house doing busywork, tidying, throwing out, more bags for the Goodwill. I am not a packrat— the things I save I generally use. I have—and still wear—the green pin- striped skirt that was part of my mother's waitress uniform at a resort on Vermont's Lake Bomoseen during her college summers nearly sixty years ago. I open boxes and cut rope with the curvy knife my paternal grandfather once used to kill pigs on his little riverside farm. But there are enough other things around this place that I wouldn't miss, and I'm culling daily, needing to reduce, simplify, get down to what is really necessary and important.

"Maybe if you worked in an office this time would be easier," some- body offers in an e-mail. "Your mind would be off your problems. It can't be good to be home alone so much." Maybe so, but this is where I am now. When my father died, I took two weeks off with the excuse that I had to help my mother with legalities and such. But a lot of it was just not wanting to be around people. That whole out-in-the-world thing seeming so surreal and scary. When I returned to the paper, my first assignment was to cover a selectmen's meeting, and I found I could not even enter the room. I stayed in the hall to make my notes, and left as soon as possible. I can't say that I'm happy right now being home alone, but I am happy not to have to be anywhere but here.

When I'm not cleaning, I work on editing next year's book, which consists of going over the comments on each page and making any changes that might improve the writing and story. It's absorbing, but I can only do so much at a time. A paragraph, some days. Or a paragraph, then a long stare out the window, downstairs to make another pot of tea, outside to see how much the trees have grown since the last time I was there about five minutes ago, then another paragraph. Also, I must finish writing the new novel by next July, and its pages are still only in double digits. That book sits waiting in its place in the computer, its characters frozen in time; the small progression I've made into their stories has them stalled in early-introduction, so they really don't know each other at all and I've stranded them with one another. Ironically, I am writing about a palm-reader, a person who can open a stranger's hand and give some idea of what the future might hold. I'd been reading about this practice, had collected a couple of books containing fascinating maps to the many areas of the palm and the information that can be divined. I know the location of the head line, the heart line and the all-important lifeline, which seems to be the one about which I've gotten the most questions when I mention I've been learning about palm-reading. Next second, people are shoving their hands toward me—"How long am I gonna live? How long am I gonna live?" Everybody wants to know this, and you can't blame them. Even when I see a short line, I answer that they'll live ages, because, really, I am no professional. And I also don't want to ruin somebody's day.

My lifeline appears to be long and deep. Which is a good thing, according to the books. Even better would be the double lifeline, which I've found on a few people. This is a cat's nine lives and an angel on your shoulder all at the same time, a field of four-leaf clovers from which you can pick again and again. Solid reassurance that no matter what the obstacle, you can—and you will—endure. Which I'd imagine to be a pretty welcoming guarantee to find etched onto your person after carrying it around your whole life and never knowing. It's been great news to the people I've found wearing this. They've walked away happy with the fascinating new knowledge, staring at the line that is no more than a simple arc. But one that spells something more. And there's that word again: hope.

# ❧ 16 ❧

I go to the courthouse with Margaret, to sit with her while she gets her divorce.

On a lovely June day eighteen years ago, I attended her wedding down in Rhode Island, Margaret's childhood home. The reception was back here in Massachusetts, at a hall that later was turned into a funeral parlor, one that I've visited only once, after a very nice friend's very nice husband fell asleep at the wheel. He loved baseball caps and his collection was on display at the wake. His son, about seven, was there as well, having made it through the crash, and walking around in a little jacket and tie. Everybody at the wake was tearfully marveling that he'd made it through. That he'd lived. Back when the place was still a reception hall, people in that building were much happier. Margaret and Larry were much happier. I was much happier. At the post-wedding bash, everybody was gone drunk. Larry followed that pattern a lot of their marriage. Was abusive physically and mentally. Harmful to her and their three children. Eighteen years after the ceremony at St. Joseph's, and the reception at the future funeral home, Margaret's well rid of him.

Except for my brief, daily appearance at radiation oncology, I have not been out in regular mainstream life for a couple of months. And I can't for the life of me think of what to wear. Especially to a divorce, something I've never attended. As a reporter, I'd sometimes have to cover a proceeding in this area of the courthouse, I'd seen its corridors of huddled half-families, and the glares being shot, and the weeping. But I can't on this day remember what anybody there had on. I end up in purple leggings and matching sweater, my high boots and my shiny red vinyl coat. Margaret has been counseled to dress conservatively, which is a switch for her, and has decided on a black skirt that extends past her knees, and a roomy blazer. Standing next to her, there in the hallway outside Courtroom 2, I look like a Kmart-sale hooker.

At the divorce hearing, you must give the reason you are seeking dissolution. As we wait, Margaret's lawyer coaches her: "In two lines or less, give the reason you feel your marriage is irreconcilable." It's like an essay contest, the big prize life without a maniac. Margaret asks, "Do I talk about his drinking and what he did?" She's informed that most people just say they grew apart and their values changed. That's if you don't want to get into anything at this point, this final day, it's not really going to change anything if you start in about the bad stuff. The lawyer's advice is to just exit your situation as quickly as you can.

Once we get into the courtroom, there are lots of other people facing this fill-in-the-blank part. Standing with his hands linked in front of him like he's handcuffed, Mr. Vasquez tells the judge, "We fell out of love and had other friends," and Mrs. Vasquez, by her request soon to return to legally being Miss Dalmer, rolls her eyes. When it is Margaret's turn, she does what makes her Margaret. She is solid and kind. She has her chance to continue, and she could have, telling horrible stories that I would know were not exaggerated in the least because I've heard them and I'm sure she's spared me a couple too awful to put into sentences. She tells the judge nothing more than, "We grew apart and our values changed."

Back in the entrance hall, a man calls out to a woman passing by with a gang of what appears to be her nearly identical sisters. They are large and good-postured and have their meanest countenances on. They surround the newly divorced woman like tugs around a freighter. The man yells, "I'll go to jail before I give you a dime!" And the woman at the center of the pack responds without turning, "I'd love ta see ya in jail." In the wake of the flotilla, Margaret is moving airily down the hall and through the dreamstate of what she just did. So I make the immediate decisions. We'll go here for lunch, park there, sit here, order this, try and relax. Her eyes are very big and she's asking me if that was it. It's over, right? Throughout the years of their problems, every time she'd stand up to Larry or throw him out, and when she at last got him out of the house for good two years ago, she'd ask me again and again, "Am I doing the right thing?" And I'd always answer that she was. The rightness of it was as big as the solar system. But she had a hard time seeing that. When you are used to poor treatment, it starts wearing another adjective: normal. She grew up in an alcoholic home, went on to another as an adult. When she wanted to change her situation, as bad as it got, she held doubt. Today, she doesn't ask me if it was the right thing. She just wants to be reassured that that truly was it, that everything is over.

I say that everything is—except for the shopping. And after lunch I drive her to T. J. Maxx, therapy for the divorced and the diseased. She complies when I instruct her to try on the cashmere sweater. She'll take that leather skirt, too, and a midnight blue brassiere that costs what I pay for a month of electricity. Everything is modeled and admired and approved, newness from the foundation on out. For me, she picks out a black fleece scarf with beads at the ends. I drape it around my neck after it clears the cash register. I drop Margaret back at the house that is now in her name. I head off to the hospital.

In this waiting room, my purple and red plumage left in the locker room, I sit in the gown covered by the blue sweatshirt and I play the songs for a lead-lined room. Earlier, I'd been waiting with a bunch of soon-to-be-divorced people. Now I'm waiting with a bunch of soon-to-be-radiated people. Between the two groups, I see little change of expression. They are all tired, sick of it, waiting for the day when everything will be over and they can get on with their lives.

A woman I've noticed here only a few times sleeps in her chair. I want to follow suit. I'm feeling more and more tired as time goes on. This was in the booklet—you'd get tired. Of course, I didn't think fatigue would get *me*. I was in shape, healthy and fit before this. I take maybe one nap a year, when a bad flu whams me, and then the sleep is due to something like Nyquil. Other than that, I never saw a reason to waste daylight in that way. Now naps are anticipated, savored. In the chair in the waiting room in the deep-down floor, I close my eyes. The ocean song starts. I float away. Annette finds me and the sea recedes into the carpet. I follow her down the hall.

# ❦ 17 ❦

The Mother's Day that I was in the eighth grade and not yet into the practice of wearing seat belts, a car accident shot me into the windshield of my parents' royal blue Plymouth Fury III, and then into a hospital bed for ten days.

The injuries leveled me for the rest of the spring and the entire summer. Patiently driving me back from yet another doctor's appointment in one of those months, my mother suggested I use my budding writing talents to tell my story in *Reader's Digest,* which back then was running a series of articles on personal challenges. I remember we were in a line of traffic at the red light near the Arby's Roast Beef on Boston Road. As we sat, the aroma of the sizzling, dripping, roasting beef wafting through the open car window was torturing: I had a jaw broken in five places and a mouth wired tight shut while those places healed up, and was existing on strawberry McDonald's milkshakes laced with protein powders, and jars of Gerber's strained pears. Making me feel worse was my mother's well-intentioned idea. How could she even think of such a thing? I did not consider myself a good patient. I had no bravery to write of, no obstacle faced with an unwavering smile. I whined about my state. Complained. Cried. Hated the doctors. Hated the rest periods. Hated the attention from visitors. I was thirteen then, I'm forty-one now. And I'm feeling that way again. Though obviously this time I am not letting that stop me from writing about it. I am still not a good patient. Sure, I do what I'm supposed to do, as far as appointments and medicine and all, but I don't go around feeling this is a challenge, a life-changing event, something to make something out of. I didn't want cancer. I don't want cancer.

"Styles vary when coping with cancer."

Tommy had ripped this story from *USA Today* and hands it to me, and I read it and I thank him, as I thank Jimmie Holland, who is chairwoman of the department of psychiatry and behavioral sciences at Memorial Sloan-Kettering Cancer Center in New York City, and who is the focus of the story, and who told the newspaper, and who is telling me, "There is an expectation in our society right now that if you get a diagnosis of cancer, you have to think positive. How can you think positive when you are upchucking from cancer? Yes, a positive attitude is good, but to say that you have to be that way all the time isn't helpful."

I want to copy this story and hire a plane and scatter reams of it onto the world. I thank Tommy again. So many things spinning in my mind. At the kitchen table just before he left for work the other day, I delayed him for most of an hour to describe this image I keep getting:

You know how sometimes when you're driving on the highway you see these soldiers in trucks? They're rolling along in front of you, part of a big convoy. Reservists, weekend warriors. They're dressed in their soldier outfits, camouflage, and they have protective helmets on and they're going along, seated in the backs of their trucks and there's a little door at the end of the truck that keeps them safely in. The top half of the door is open to the air and sometimes the soldiers look out and wave as you're passing or following. You don't know where they're going, and maybe they don't either. But they appear to be having a good time nonetheless.

Six months ago I didn't know where I was going. I was having a good time. I was having a good life. And then the door at the end of the truck bed swung open and I tumbled onto the road and the truck kept going. Now I have no idea where I am. I don't know how to go on. Where am I supposed to be? I'm in the middle of the road and I'm banged up and dazed and now what? I was having a good time. I was having a good life.

"You were having a good time for too long," Margaret told me in her little pantry as she was getting out the cups and I just by chance got handed the one that reads *Snap Out of It*. She laughed. Coming from almost anybody else I might have been hurt. But she's right in a way. I was having a good time, and it did go on for a long time. But what's wrong with that? Now I'm down here on the hard old road, and I have no idea, and the truck is not coming back for me. I know it is never going to. I have to go on from here by myself. And that feels very lonely. I ask Tommy if he understands this, does the story I told him make sense to him. He says it does, of course it does, he adds in reassurance. But I know that he had his own road onto which he was dumped on the night when I got the diagnosis out of the nurse. And even if I want to try, I can't fathom where he landed—just as he can't fully understand where I am now. We are both alone, together. My head feels that. The house does, too. A big place, but our chatter and my making things and his music and a dog's four hairy paws shuffling along always seemed to fill it up with energy. There's something hanging over us all now, and it's pressed the mute button on almost everything. I was always a great one for feeling guilty even about things that happened before I was born, and now I am in high gear, feeling that because the disease is in me, though I did not send an invitation, it is my fault. And how it has affected me has affected Tommy—and there's a whole other life negatively impacted. I cause concern in my mother and in Cindy and in people I don't even know who are taking the time to kneel down and pray. A big wide circle I can feel lousy about, and I am very good at that. "I'm sorry," I tell Tommy. "I'm sorry." And he says again, it is not my fault.

Radiation oncology is fairly littered with offers of what patients can do to help themselves get better, feel better. All those classes and courses and workshops and specialists. I see little, if anything, aimed at family. Who helps the family? There is another news story I find relevant. Somebody rips it out for Tommy and he offers it to me, if I want to read it, which I already had, because this topic bothers me. There is little to no attention given the loved ones of women with breast cancer.

"What's happened to our wonderful, stable life?" That is the question the men are asking in this story. The women have to be asking it, too, but this is not about them. This is about the men who don't know what to do—thrown from the truck onto their own lonely road.

Right now it's me me me. But what about him him him?

Tommy returned from a gathering recently to tell me everybody was asking for me. One person, the quietest, the most inarticulate in the group, took him aside and asked, "How do you feel?" With the emphasis on the you, the him, the Tommy. And that hit Tommy enough so that he mentioned it several times to me. That somebody would acknowledge him. And would without saying it understand that there are scars from this on him, too.

In these past months I've often wondered how it would feel to be the well one watching the other tread through an illness. Tommy has always been extremely patient and understanding, but he's also always known who I am. That's no longer really so. I've changed, and I continue to change. The playing field seems to shift as I have good or bad days. The rules I set change without notice. He does his best to endure my moods and crying jags, to figure out whether or not this is a morning on which he can offer a hug, listen intently to my newest take on the meaning of life, attempt to answer questions that don't have answers.

There have been rougher times during this, arguments over and dissections of healthcare decisions, everyday actions, poorly chosen words. Afterward, grudges drift threateningly at the edges of these issues and it is tempting to remain silent rather than discuss what is eating you alive. I miss the same wonderful, stable life the guy in the newspaper article was mourning. None of this life now is very pretty, and is the type of scene left on the cutting room floor when they make those disease movies.

≈≈≈

Work and the baseball team provide Tommy a regular healthy distance and break from me. If I were him, I'd take on a second and third job just to have more time away. If I were him, I would be nowhere near as kind as he's been. And I'm not just saying that. In the middle of all this, I get a peek at the view from the other side of the fence when Tommy undergoes surgery for kidney stones.

Pain drove him out of bed at five in the morning and soon I was driving him to my town's hospital, where he would spend the day hurting, and in panic over his first-ever surgical procedure. Nothing I said alleviated his fears over how bad his experience might be, worries that included would they knock him out enough to not feel anything. By the time he was wheeled into the operating room in late afternoon, I found I'd taken on a lot of his anxiety, but I also found myself hungry. Cindy and David were there, wanting to know what could they do. "Dinner?" I asked.

My husband had kept vigil in the hospital waiting room while I had my surgery. As the doctor was snaking a variety of lengthy instruments up Tommy's penis and beyond, I tucked into a heaping plate of onion rings in Friendly's. We returned in time to see him delivered back to his bed and to get the good word from the doctor, who proclaimed the operation a success and called the trio of stones he held out to us in a plastic jar the largest he'd ever removed. "I'm gonna keep these on my desk," he informed us as Tommy slept off the anesthesia while I just wanted to get out of there.

# ❧ 18 ❧

Cindy stayed the night. She didn't want me to be alone. We fixed tea and she fell asleep next to me on the couch, in a seated position. I led her up to the spare bed and found my own. I had no trouble sleeping. Shouldn't I have tossed, or at least turned? My husband operated on, record-setting things removed from him through a portal you would rather not have invaded, and now drugged and hospitalized? Maybe so, but I didn't. I fell asleep quickly and woke when Cindy did, way too early, found her some suitable office clothing and sent her off for another day at the UMass office of administration and finance.

I phoned the hospital. Tommy was up, and retrievable, so I drove over and sat with him until his release time. In a johnny and in a bed with railings, whiter than usual and hair flattened from its usual Lyle Lovett skyward explosion, he looked like a genuine sick person. For his part, he said he felt miles better than the day before. I confessed my trip to Friendly's, as well as my good rest. Neither of those things bothered him. "Good for you," he said, which is what he always says when I do something that is not for the benefit of somebody else—pleasing others having been for most of my life my codependentish motivation and aim. Whenever I do something I might think of as selfish, Tommy cheers me on, says good for you. Now he is saying, let's go home, and

I help him into a sweatsuit and he is wheeled to the front door and I bring his car around and because I'm nervous and because I'm not used to driving an automatic I don't move the shift after I park and the car begins to roll when I get out. "Hey!" a woman on crutches yells from the sidewalk, and I chase the car and jump in the open door and slam on the brakes. The ride home is uneventful. I install Tommy in front of ESPN with blanket and pillow and a bottle of water and go to fill his prescription, another thing he's done for me.

⋙⋘

At the other hospital I go to, on this same day, Luz is looking happier. Her final treatment is tomorrow. It can't come soon enough for her. She says she's been throwing up daily for the last month. They are not aiming the radiation at her stomach, so why is this? She wants to know. She asks me. I don't know either.

"I feel terrible," she tells me. "And I can't even wear my brassiere. Got big black marks." I don't know anything about black marks. My skin is getting only a little pink, a little day-at-the-topless-beach. I must appear puzzled because Luz opens her gown and invites "Lookit." And there's her baked right breast, looking like the blackened salmon Tommy orders whenever we hit Bub's Barbecue. My eyes shoot away. I don't want to see this. If that is what happens here, I don't want to know ahead of time.

Other than increasing fatigue, the side effect I'm really starting to notice is one some people would pay for: I'm not that hungry. This was also in the radiation booklet: "You might lose your appetite." Might, might, might. I did. Another first. I've always loved to eat, always left a plate so clean it could be put right back on the shelf without a trip under the faucet. I never had a problem, even in time of crisis. Except for this one. Cindy is astounded because, for the first time since we met, I'm offering her my leftovers.

People don't like to hear that you aren't interested in eating. So they are kindly researching what I need. Printing out from the Internet, lending books, relaying what was testified about by nutty callers on 3 A.M. radio talk shows. My mother brings more soup. My mother-in-law uses one of her coupons and buys me a little flip-top can of liquid that is supposed to contain all the nutrients necessary for one day. That efficiency is no tradeoff for its decidedly barium-enema-prep taste. Tea is recommended right now. Not my preferred black—in this state I'm supposed to be drinking green tea for its ability to inhibit the COX-2 enzyme that allows cancerous cells to grow. At least that's what's printed on the side of the box of green tea my pal Jeannie leaves on the porch next to a big and pretty tea cup. I don't know what a COX-2 enzyme is. But apparently it knows who I am. Found me. Did its thing. In retaliation against cancer, I brew a cup.

Thankfully, nobody leaves any on my GO AWAY mat, but I'm told fatty fish are the way to go. Salmon, mackerel, eel, tuna, halibut, cod, sardines. They are said to inhibit the body's ability to make prosta-glandins, in this way stopping breast cancer cell growth. Ten years ago I stopped eating anything with a face or a mother. And even on my most carnivorous day I wouldn't have dreamed of putting an eel on my plate. So that's out. Easier is the cruciferous route. Broccoli, brussels spouts, cabbage, stuff I've always liked, and did long before I read they are high in indole-3-carbinole, another thing said to prevent the bad cells from flourishing like the scary begonias in a Miracle-Gro com-mercial. But if you don't feel like eating anything, even the best-looking produce is nothing more than a subject for a still life. I do paint, but I don't feel like painting. These days, the creative wave is limited to the little space between my returning home from the hospital and going for a nap, and, now, seeing what I can do for Tommy. In that slim little canyon, I sit here and I write my day.

# ~ 19 ~

It's Luz's last treatment.

When I walk into the waiting room, I find her seated on the side opposite from where she usually is. And right next to the lamp. I go over and tell her I think it's wonderful that she's done and I hope she stays well, and good luck. We hug. She is smiley and teary and nods her response. I leave because Annette quickly calls me for my turn and I exit so fast that I startle myself. I leave Luz there and even as I do I instantly regret not saying what I was thinking. Which was, the first day I waited in this room, I could not even look at you. I couldn't because I didn't know what to do for you, or if I should do anything. It bothered me to be here. It bothered me that you were upset. I remember saying to Cindy, well, I don't know whether or not to chat somebody up in there, how to respond if they're being emotional—I don't know what to say to these people. And she replied with a potent: "You know, don't you—you are 'these people.' "

When I'm back in the hallway after my time on the machine, Luz is gone. I'll probably never see her again. I no longer see the other person I was getting used to running into here, the art therapist who wore the silver shoes and the camouflage socks and the stick-figure earrings and the cloth scapular sticking out from the front of her gown like the pull chain for a forcefield. From her lack of hair, it was pretty evident she had gone through chemotherapy as well. When I got my diagnosis and phoned Cindy, I eventually tried to make light and joked that this would have to happen just when my hair was at a good length. I thought chemotherapy was a given. The drugs eventually gave Cindy a Sinead O'Connor look that miraculously since then has led to a headful of curls for a woman who'd had straight strands her entire life. I have not cut my hair for eleven months, but just because I never got around to it. It's getting long. People tell me that, as if I don't know. "Your hair's getting long," they say. And, "You look skinny." But most often I hear, "You don't look sick." Which is good.

I don't feel sick. Maybe I don't want the party-size pizza, maybe I'm in bed more than out of it, but I don't feel sick. But neither do I feel like the me I've always known. The way I was in the life I'd like to have back.

My surgeon visited me at 8 A.M. the morning after the lumpectomy. I had the blankets up over my head like a corpse, but more due to the extreme air-conditioning than any morbid thoughts.

He said my name and I pulled down the covers and he asked how I was and then he checked the dressing and then he told me I could go home that morning and I could resume normal activities in two days.

He said it just like that: "You can resume normal activities in two days."

And I'm thinking, great! That big bridal shower for Christine was to be the following Sunday. Two weeks after that, a Saw Doctors concert I'd been anticipating. It was early August and the summer was in glorious full swing. In two days I'd be rejoining it, out on the river again, hiking the woods, lying on the roof outside my bedroom to watch a meteor shower or just moonbathe.

Well, I had the lying part right. Two days later I was still flat on my back, icepack shoved into my armpit, scooping up painkillers like coffee table cashews. A couple of days after that, the scene wasn't much different. As I said, I never made it to Christine's shower. I did get to the concert, but Cindy had to drive me, and we sat in lawn chairs near the back entrance and drank tea from a thermos like convalescent-home residents on a day pass. My progress was slow. I could not use the kayak for another month. My hikes weren't much more than to and from the mailbox across the street. I didn't like any of it.

"Does that doctor know what your idea of 'normal activities' is?"

Susan asked this. Since getting sibling setters two summers before, she and I walked nearly every afternoon with our dogs. Leo is mine. Riley is Susan's. The dogs knew each other from the first minute, being two of fourteen puppies born to a Gordon setter mother and an English setter father. As for the humans' history, Susan and I have lived four minutes away from each other for fifteen years but met only a couple of Junes back. The following weekend, she greeted into her family nine-week-only Riley, and I adopted Leo the next Sunday. The four of us have been together on the same path ever since, Susan and I becoming fast friends, our relationship formed and fostered, and continuing to thrive, on the move. On the walks we've taken three or four times a week since the dogs were puppies.

She's a painter, and because both of us work at home we easily find a break in our days to exercise "the kids," as Susan calls them. So that's what we do, regularly stretching the legs of humans and canines, sweeping out the minds of all.

Through the woods and fields, and along the rivers of our small town, we've tromped behind the dogs and have introduced ourselves to each other through mile-long monologues, telling the stories and drawing the pictures of our lives. We've walked backward into the sand-whipping wind on May beaches, mucked home in sudden bucketing July downpours, shuffled through big snow beneath January full moons. All with the dogs charging alongside and past us. The day before my surgery, Susan helped me dye my hair for the first time. Cindy had shared with me that the majority of her visitors post-surgery had looked at her chest before her face, and she suggested I be prepared for that. I got the idea that a new haircolor would get them looking elsewhere for a time, and Susan accompanied me down the CVS aisle, where we decided on a shade of red found nowhere in nature. She also joined me in the coloring, and then a dog-walk to let it set. We wandered a bit too far and left the stuff on a little too long, and the result was more than sufficient.

"Your hair!" visitors would cry.

"Side effect," I'd deadpan.

⋙⋘

I don't walk half as much anymore. And it shows on Leo, if nowhere else. She's not a house dog, but she's become one, sleeping on my bed every time I do, which is happening more often as the treatments add up. She is not a housedog. I am not a houseperson. But here I am, at home, with Susan's Go Away mat at the back door, waiting to feel up to resuming my normal activities. To resuming normal life.

"Somebody always has it worse." How many times have you heard that? How many times have I? And, you know what? It's true. I've seen it. Both from just being a person on the planet, and also from my newspaper work, a rare front-seat ticket to events good and bad. I wrote often about these bad things, interviewed the victims or, failing that opportunity, the survivors. Did the follow-ups to find how everyone was doing or not doing, a week or a month or a year after whatever had ripped their lives in half. I saw things. Police exhuming the body of a missing child from the shallow wooded grave in which she'd been discovered. High schoolers in ill-fitting adult suits and heels trudging zombielike to three successive funerals after their classmates sped down a road, then suddenly off it. A man crumpled to the ground and asking aloud where would he live now, as the wet black flakes of debris that you would never know are in the smoke of a housefire rained on him. A lovely funny woman my age smiling hopefully as the photographer shot the picture that would run with the piece on her desperate search for a bone-marrow donor—the same photo used when I wrote of her death.

I saw this, as well: a lot of the good stuff that people always complain there is not enough of in the newspaper. One of the first stories I did after being hired fulltime was the wedding of Norman and Ruth, a couple who had in common their love, and also their cerebral palsy, their wheelchairs and their caring home aids who whisked them away on a seaside honeymoon. Over the years I covered the graduations of proud, fist-pumping, fomerly "at risk" students whom everyone but the school staff had abandoned long before. Generous gardeners who donated their backyard produce to senior centers and food pantries, benevolent town groups that funded the purchase of service dogs and monuments and scholarships and sports uniforms. Disparate neighborhoods that banded together to fight plans for a landfill or mega-retailer in their town. Adoptions of tossed-aside kids whose new parent-angels were their only hope. The return home of a optimistic young doctor who'd spent an eye-opening internship on a remote reservation. And one Christmas I wrote about my friend Joe Bigda, who each December lights up, on the steep hill above his village, four enormous hand-built letters that spell out HOPE.

What I've been privileged and disturbed to witness in my life, all of it has been like the soups I'd watch my mother make, ingredients chopped and added and stirred and simmered together, and the result has been the desire to wrap my arms around the planet, to congratulate it, to soothe it, to say it'll be OK. Normally I am as optimistic as the slogans in which I now find solace. But the cancer has invaded that as well, and I am unnaturally self-absorbed and down, critical enough to pick on Tommy's own mouth-gaping about how his seemingly healthy body can just up and do something that requires drastic measures, making him no more than a rank amateur whiner when I start listing my woes. But when I hear something about Molly Bish, I feel awful for making such a big deal about what is happening to me me me. Yesterday, her family appeared on Sally Jessy Raphael. Tonight they joined three hundred or so supporters who lined up for a benefit supper at Old Mill Pond School, where Magdalen teaches. They can go on TV.

They can sit in public and eat ham and beans with a bunch of strangers who want nothing more than to help. Me, I hide from the postman, who is such a nice guy he has taken to bringing the mail to the back door even where there is no big envelope or package to require that special service.

# ❧ 20 ❧

The month is half over. It has the pace of a caterpillar. One that stops a lot, to examine something.

I have never known time to pass so slowly. The treatments will last somewhere into the beginning of November. That seems like California, and to get there I must walk, starting from here in Massachusetts.

It is the full moon. My favorite night of the month. I love the moon at all times—simply the fact we have one. It's something that probably every person who ever existed and had working eyes got to see at least once. Think about that. I know the sun is there every day, but you really can't stare at that for hours. Plus the sun doesn't have those fantastic metaphor-packed phases: bummer, it's getting smaller and everything's getting darker and bleaker and, hey, where'd that one light in all that blackness go? But—wait—look! Here it comes again. Larger and more powerful as the month goes on, until the big night and the big light and you can stand outside and read the classifieds if you want. Oooh, just like life. . . .

I like to wait until it's high in the sky, late at night. Then I go to the river and float in the miracle of it. But for some, the full moon isn't such a peaceful experience. Annette tells me it's a tough time of the month for dealing with the public, and, like clockwork, on this day she gets screamed at by a patient. He warns that he will come and get her off-hours. She is upset because during her bartender years she was stalked. It was an ordeal, she tells me. She does not want to go through that again. Recurrence would be the medical word for this. I am learning such terms. Whether it's being followed by a crazy person or having something grow inside you once again, it's the same term. And the same fright, I'd imagine. Sure, you're done with something, it's over and it's happened already, but there is no guarantee it won't take place again.

≈≈

I go to see my general practioner. Having a prescription for the country's number-one antidepressant requires that you check in periodically and report how you're feeling and doing.

"Are you taking care of yourself?" he wants to know. "Getting any exercise?"

With no transition or pause, the doctor says he remembers when he was having a difficult time and his communication with God ducked behind a cloud, just as mine has. He leans back in his chair when he begins this. We are in for a long reminiscence. He says it happened ten years ago. No, fifteen. No, maybe ten. . . . The intercom buzzes to say a patient is on the phone. "Yeah, OK," says the doctor, and he goes on to tell me how when he was having a difficult time and not feeling like going to mass he shared that fact with a priest and the priest said to him, "Do you think God gives a shit whether or not you go to mass? He doesn't care." Then the intercom buzzes again. The patient is still on the line. And now the pharmacy, too. "What does she want?" he asks about the patient. "Something about her arm," the nurse says. "Oh," the doctor says, and he releases the intercom button and he takes a slug from the two-liter bottle of Adirondack seltzer on his blotter and he asks me, "You know that God gives a shit about you, don't you?"

I do know that God gives a shit. Whether or not you stop by his house at the appointed hour each week. From childhood I've held this image given to me by Sister Tobia, the nun I had for first and second grades. She told the rows and rows of us that if God wasn't thinking of you, you would disappear. Poof. Nothing would be left of you. Just like that. Air in the ancient wooden desk still with its inkwell hole, nothing but nothing where you once were seated in your little navy blue jumper with the Ss. Peter and Paul SPPS patch and the Sodality of Mary pin on the left breast, smack over the place where you will one day have a crescent moon of a scar. So right now, if you are here typing this, or you are there reading this, according to what Sister Tobia said, God is thinking of you. To use the doctor's terms, He gives a shit. But the rhyme or reason of the rest of life's mysteries, who can figure that out? Molly is still missing. There is still not a single clue. Tim Kargol is still dead. The flowers on his grave have wilted and have been removed. I am still here. I am not having an easy time right now, but I am still here.

# ❧ 21 ❧

Holly wants to take me on a foliage ride. Not my guru's smiling intern, Holly from the hospital, Holly from the paper. We used to work together while covering our respective little towns and at some point or other, Holly has covered all those I was once assigned to—Belchertown, Monson, Brimfield, West Brookfield, as well as Warren, which includes the tiny village of West Warren, home to the Bish family. We skirt that town on this Saturday, as we head to do the touristy thing of visiting an orchard.

I've never been to this particular one, despite having seen its apple-shaped signs nailed to trees for years. It's like the house with the display of perennials for sale on the way to the hospital—you honestly mean to stop there one day, but never do. This orchard is old, but they've jazzed it up with a kitchen in the barn that turns out racks and racks of pies, cakes, and cookies. The yard has picnic tables for enjoying what you carry out on a paper plate, and there is also a petting zoo, and a big wagon pulled by an old tractor that takes visitors on tours of the orchard. Holly and I get pie slices and sit at the tables. Yellowjackets dive-bomb us from their buzzing headquarters at the trash can. Behavior you'd expect from flies, not bees, but they are not ones to play by the rules, it seems, doing whatever they want simply because who's going to stop them? We move and find some peace. The sun is summer-warm, as if fall made a mistake and began too early. The pie is perfect and reminds me of childhood and the apples out back and my mother rolling crusts for the slices she's cut from the bushels we've just picked. Kids abandon their harassment of the chickens and the ponies and throw themselves onto the wagon and the tractor is put into gear by a teenage boy in a straw hat he doesn't seem to be wearing for any corny-farm effect but only because he needs to wear a hat in this sun. Life is buzzing, yelling, growing, moving all around our picnic table. I decide I need another piece of pie.

Next we stop at an arts festival in Monson. Paintings, photographs, prints, reliefs hang from fences and display boards. Holly has an eye for art and she stops at a printmaker's small etchings and considers two for the walls of the home she's decorating with great care. I wander and come upon the display of Evelyn, whom both Holly and I have written about at some point along the way, Evelyn being a Monson resident and a painter and gardener and all-around nice person to cover if she's in a show and you must write something about one of the people in it. Evelyn is of my grandmother's era, recently was widowed, and has been up against a few health adventures of her own, including one that affects her speech. But there she is, seated against a fence hung with her paintings of New Englandy scenes, beaches, gardens, showing off her latest creations and chatting with those who pass. Half an hour away, at the newspaper's main building, my friend Howard edits copy and puts together the front page for the big Sunday edition. A couple of years ago, over a few short months, he lost his sight. A hereditary thing with no hope for repair. The paper obtained a special computer screen and he's in front of that today, doing his work, going about his life. Howard and I are around the same age. I one day would like to be Evelyn's age. And both now and later, I'd like to have a measure of whatever it is that keeps them moving on.

# ☙ 22 ❧

I need to get to the CVS for more of the country's number-one antidepressant. Tommy is reading his usual stack of Sunday papers, and I ask him if he'd like to come along. I surprise him by making the offer, and I surprise myself. We haven't been doing that much together lately, and a lot of that is my fault, some of it being my feeling I'm on another planet right now, and some of it being my reaction to his reaction to his operation. I never said you'd find my face framed next to that of Mother Teresa, and here is another reason why not: every time he talks to someone now, up comes the subject of the kidney stones. How painful they were, how he had to wait the entire day to have the surgery, how the things turned out to be imbedded and infected and—did he mention?—the biggest ones the doctor had ever seen? I can almost stand aside with amazement as I watch myself get incensed over his simply telling his friends what happened. He has every right to complain, what he went through was no fun at all, and it scared him a great deal because he's never had anything wrong with him. Yet it annoys me that he goes on and on about it. Comes home from work to say he found another two guys in the city room who'd had kidney stones, and how they were commiserating with him, and also agreeing with the doctor that there is no real way you can say it will never happen again.

Chances are, any given day you'll be back on the floor again, pain so bad you'll feel you're going to die. "It's true," Tommy tells me. "There is really nothing they can do about it. I'm just a stone maker, the doctor says." I say that sounds like the name of a rock—no pun intended— group. I don't want to say what I'm really thinking, partly because I don't want to start a fight, and mostly because it is embarrassing after all the whining I've been doing these past six months. But I cannot get over his preoccupation with the kidney stones and the hospital experience and his reciting for the fiftieth time where the doctor had to insert the instrument. I want to say that they are only kidney stones. What would happen to you if you had something worse than that? Maybe I know the answer. Maybe he'd be acting just like me.

We go to the CVS and then I ask if he wants to go to the orchard I visited the day before. It's another day that is like a big postcard you would mail to impress someone who's never seen your corner of the world, plus there is pie at this place. So we go. The tractor is taking off, but we walk the orchard instead, tracing the path around its edge, where the woods begin and the grass is highest. He takes my hand and I feel as if we're on a date. That we need to get to know each other, and that there will be a lot to learn once we do get started. I get sad. All the beauty makes me feel this way. Things so bright in the world and within me a darkness. We get to a field, I hold onto him and cry. Then I think how the cart of apple pickers will be coming by any second, all happy, this is their big day out and look at us here. Somebody's always in pain. That is the way of the world. Except you would prefer to skip that reality if you could, and never have to be anybody else but the person removed from it, sitting in a tractor cart having nothing to do with the problem, free to turn your head from any unpleasant scene and look instead at the rows of Macouns and Empires and Golden Delicious.

I once visited a seaside resort area that many people had described to me as a big carefree holiday party place, and the first thing I saw after I parked the car was a man sitting on the rocks, sobbing. He wore a dress shirt and tie and he looked suited up for the office and he was on the boulders near the water in his misery. I wanted to go over to him and say it'll be OK, even though I had no idea of his problem. I'm on my holiday, and there he is in his reality. He's another Luz. I don't know what to do. Again, I do nothing.

All around me here in this orchard, the apples are like grapes on the trees, in heavy huge clusters, dusty with pesticide. When you pass a tree, an apple will fall and bang on the ground. When I first hear this, I think that somebody is throwing them. Then I realize things have to fall when they have to fall.

# ❦ 23 ❦

Monday. Back to work. Fourth week on the job.

I'm walking across the little driveway between the parking lot and the hospital and a van comes flying along way too fast and it has to slam on the brakes or it'll hit me. I'm suddenly rooted in the road, incredulous. This is about twenty feet from the exit where people are leaving the building with their brand-new babies. There also are lots of older folks passing through here, and in-patients in their wheelchairs, smoking, hooked up to IVs, hobbling on walkers. It's not the best place to be speeding.

When I do move from my spot in the center of the road, the van guns past me and the driver sneers. It is a Baystate van. I memorize the license plate when he slows to flirt with the female valet who's always nice to me. At the information desk just inside the door, I ask the volunteer for a pen and I write down the plate, which I've been repeating in my head, on a copy of a hospital map. There is a guard standing right there, as if anticipating me, killing time and waiting for a chance to bring some security to the world. I say I have work for him, that he should go and tell this driver to slow down. I give him the plate information. I tell him I don't come here to be treated for cancer just so I can get killed by one of their vans.

"I know you," says the older of the two volunteers at the desk, pointing. I recognize her, the mother of a friend, and I used to run into her all the time when I worked out at the Figures and Fitness salon soon after I started at the paper. The deal was six weeks for twenty-five dollars. Each time you entered, they'd make you get on the scale and they'd weigh you and mark your weight on a card, and if you lost a pound they'd ring a little bell so all your fellow women would be aware that somebody in there was making progress toward her goal. One afternoon I told the attendant not to ring the bell because I thought it demeaning, that I only went there to work out, not for applause, and she went to ring it anyhow, and I went to push it from her reach, and the entire cabinet fell over, which is more embarrassing than getting attention because of a bell. This volunteer at the hospital information desk used to go there, too. She wore about sixteen necklaces and they would get trapped in her tan cleavage when she did her aerobicizing. Now, two decades later, she is a volunteer at the hospital where I am being treated for cancer. And she's somehow come to take my hand as I'm talking with the security guard and she's telling me this hand is cold and I must be shook up and I ask her well, who wants to get almost run over? And the security man comes back all official and tells me, "He'll pay, don't worry." I say I don't want him to pay. I just want him to slow down and not kill anybody.

≈≈

In the waiting room, it's me and an old couple I've never seen. The woman is fussing over the man, who is in a wheelchair angled toward her. She's neatening his sleeves and patting his hand and there's an intimacy that makes me feel sad because this is another thing cancer does to you—makes you consider the fact that you might not be old with anybody. Anybody. I put the headphones on. I have the tape cued to the ocean song and I fall into it. My eyes rest on the wheels of the old man's chair. They're clean and shiny, right out of the wheelchair showroom. There are various gadgets attached that must allow the thing to move, and brake. I work my eyes up to the hubs. The thin spokes. The rubber tire itself. The padded armrest. The man's tan plaid shirt, which reminds me of the comfortably worn types my grandfather favored. My eyes travel to the sleeve that's being patted, the collar, and then to the man's face as he's looking at his wife and that's when I see it—the kind of marking that I have on my chest. Only his is on his temple. This man has something bad growing in his head. My eyes are now level with his wife's, and she smiles at me and the man turns to me and he smiles, too, and the both of them are saying something to me so I take off the earphones and I don't know the answer to the question I missed so I just go, "It's cold in here." And the woman tells me more than asks me, "Your hands are cold." And I say they are, and she says, "My mother, I have to go over to her and rub her hands, her hands are always cold." And I'm thinking how old is her mother, as this woman is, like, from the 1600s.

The man is one of the few I see in the waiting room. Recently, there has been a youngish guy, maybe in his thirties, dressy pants and shoes and the johnny on top. He looks out of place—most of those who are waiting here are female. Most of them are older than I am. I still check that. I also check the obits. I normally will look at the page, but now I find myself scanning for details. Ages. Cause of death, which because it is not our newspaper's style to include that, I must guess at. The agencies to which memorial contributions can be made are often the giveaway. I make note of any mentions of the American Cancer Society. The National Cancer Institute. Rays of Hope. If it's a woman whose obit mentions one of those, and they're approximately my age, I read it again. I look at the name of the husband, or the "close friend" newspapers will now include in lieu of a spouse. Any kids? Usually some of them, wearing the names of mother or father. Sometimes these women also leave grandmothers. And that's how young they can be—they are dead, yet they can still have a living grandparent. I pull together some thoughts of solace and strength to beam across the sky and blanket the home on whatever street or lane or avenue the deceased is listed as once inhabiting. I do that, and then I tell myself that God, even if I'm not always thinking of him much these days, is still thinking of me. Because here, on this page of obituaries, this list of survivors, this specified charity, this boldface surname, the still-smiling face in the outdated photograph, none of this is yet mine.

# ❦ 24 ❦

I visit Margaret most days before I go into the hospital. Just a quick hour maybe. We talk about her neck and divorce stuff and my breast and confusion stuff and we share a pot of tea and then her kids start coming home from school and ignoring her and ignoring me and that's the time at which I must leave for my appointment.

Today her back neck feels better and she plays me a song on her piano just before I go. She learned music as a child, resumed lessons in recent years, and she's very good. There is a beige upright where Larry's huge fish tank once burbled. Margaret sits with as much good posture as the instrument has. Sometimes when she masters a piece, she will call my phone and leave it on the answering machine. I'll play those recorded ones again and again. Today the music is in person. I have my coat on when she plays for me, and the black beady scarf she gave me, and I close my eyes and it's my last few minutes before being launched back into the world. I hear the melody, and it sounds like what I feel: notes plodding along their own version of slow October, not really ascending though you hope for them to do so.

❧❧

Even though I take the Walkman into the waiting room, I sometimes bring a book along as well. This day it is a library one that Susan got for me from the highest shelf. Vladimir Lange has titled his book *Be a Survivor*, as if you might choose the alternative, as if you might have a choice. I find this quote in there, from a breast cancer survivor, an older woman identified only as Imogene:

"I can't state too loudly to women with breast cancer that in order to have a fuller and richer life you need to use the rage you have creatively. If you have some talent, use it and do something with it. Get your rage out. I think that's the most important thing for survival, and for a fuller, richer life."

The word "rage" sticks out for me as if it's in neon. It is all I see. There is a surprise to that, the fact that I identify with the need for ridding myself of rage. I don't feel so much angry as I do confused—the "why" of cancer finding me still occupies too much of my mind. I copy the rage quote onto the back of an envelope containing a get-well card from an acquaintance who is the type of man you would not expect to be sending such a thing, someone who I am surprised to learn could feel anything so strongly that he would go out and pay money for a card and write not just his name inside but the fact that he was so sorry to hear about me. As I write Imogene's quote, I see that when I get to the disease name, I abbreviate it to "b.c.," which, prior to all this, would have meant prehistory to me. I remember Cindy telling me that this will be on all my medical charts from now on.

B.C.

There is a picture of Imogene next to the quote. She is smiling. She does not look enraged. I wonder what she did with hers, where it went.

I was not brought up to express anger. It was not considered polite. But maybe I am now correcting that in this experience, allowing it now for the first time in my life. Feeling the rage of this big interruption that has shoved me up against the wall and propped my eyes open. I bet that on some days, Peregrine looked down at his bloody ankle and felt rage. After all, saints are only human. As am I.

This day, I come home to another one. Saint Martha. As in Margaret's old church.

My sister-in-law Mary sends Martha to me. Another package from Ireland, this one postmarked from the town in which Mary is a hospital administrator. She's been living over there since graduating from UMass in the seventies, and comes back here once a year with a massive wheeled bag bearing Cadbury's Roses and Christy Moore CDs, vacuum-packed rashers and sausages, and all the news from West Kerry. She is independent and focused and cool and strong and I wish she lived closer. Mary has been writing to me about her novena to Martha, a powerful saint, sister of the Virgin Mary so you know she has to have great connections. The novena to Martha must be made on a long series of nine Tuesdays and involves the lighting of a candle each time. If you forget a Tuesday, you have to start all over. Mary wrote that she forgot, and she had to start over again after making good progress into the novena. It is not an easy thing.

The prayer card is inside a little plastic envelope containing a medal of Martha, who is dressed in a white gown with a blue robe over it. She is shoeless and holds a long cross, the end of which is stabbed into the mouth of an ugly sea serpent lurking behind her, rolling its eyes, curling its tail and lashing its tongue. Martha's expression is much more hopeful than Peregrine's. She intercedes, too. She overcame a dragon.

A dragon.

# ❦ 25 ❦

Annette has no time to talk. There's been a recent big increase in patients—thirty percent—and she's feeling it daily, she tells me. She's pre-
occupied and not herself. But I need her attention and her usual kindness. I'm very anxious today, and yammering on about my skin getting
burned in the manner the books predicted. I tell her that my breast is
not a place I usually worry about getting a burn. I go on about once
being on a nude beach in the West Indies, it was all great until you
heard not the island's French language but an American speaking.
Then of course you'd think it was no other American but the creepy
guy from down your street and that was a different thing altogether, to
be naked in front of someone you knew and didn't like. Annette says
"Uh-huh." She is calculating the machine and asks could I keep still,
I'm gesturing about the Americans over there behind the dune, and I
go on talking, I ask her don't you ever have younger people in here? It
continues to amaze me how I can be the youngest patient around for
miles. She tells me that cancer doesn't usually happen to people between twenty and forty. After that age, I guess, look out. I was forty-
one when I was diagnosed, just over the county line, into the land of
danger, like crossing from the happy part of some nation into the section that has yet to give up warring. "When I was diagnosed." I hear

myself saying those words to Annette. It sounds awful, and even to type it out is strange. I was diagnosed. Cancer. Type it out. Six letters. Awful. "No, you don't see young people in here," Annette says, "because the majority of the patients are older women with breast cancer, and men with prostate cancer."

I know this already. I see them in the waiting room, staring at the rug and their shoes, anyplace but the face across the way. I do try to look at people, to make contact, but I don't try too hard. My guru reminds me I might benefit from getting to know some of the others. But I haven't the energy. I'm tired and I just want to get in and out, not trade pleasantries or recipes or, as is more often the case, horror stories: "I had this, then it turned into that, then they said it was the other thing, now I got something else. It always turns into something else, you know." That's the cheery message from one woman there. The Roseanne Roseannadanna's "It's always something." I turn up the songs for the lead-lined room, and the word-picture of the ocean washes efficiently over the hopeful dreading.

My shift is now shared with three other women: a very jolly black woman always in a skirt, whose name I learn is Carvella, an old white woman with gray hair, and a much whiter white woman younger than that who naps until she's called. I feel like napping, too, and have begun to. Though when it comes to night sleeping, I'm exhausted but can't rest. Not wanting to disturb Tommy, I lie in the guest room next to Leo, who followed me in there, and I think, "I have cancer. Don't help me. Help me."

But I don't have it, not really. This is what one woman, who recently had "it" tells me. "Yours was nothing, you got off easy. You know what I had to go through?"

I do. I know. Because she told everybody who had ears. But she is thirty years older than I am. The older you get, the more illness dogs you. At seventy, you're probably going to have something, or will get it soon. For women in that decade, it's often breast cancer. At forty is another story. That's how I see it, however it sounds, and I think that is part of why I am so stunned.

"You don't really have cancer." Another woman tells me this. She is married to a doctor. He explained it to her, she says. "This is the kind the doctor is happy to tell you about." She uses the word "happy." "I mean he is not dreading it when he puts his hand on the doorknob to go and tell you the diagnosis. This is nothing. Now Cindy, she really had it. . . ."

# ⚭ 26 ⚭

Margaret's parents stop by her house en route to the airport. Her mother is a retired nurse and is asking about my health.

"What?" her father wants to know. He mis-hears and he asks, "Did you have an accident?" He's kind of a joker so I say, "Yeah, I had a big accident. I have cancer." Another pronouncement aloud, to make it true. The more I say it the more it sinks in to me and seems less like a rotten dream. Margaret's father begins to scramble for his story. Most everybody in his position does. You can see the gears turning; they have to say something to fill up the space after hearing the word.

Early on in this, I was struck by the reactions. I'd tell people about the cancer. The look they'd get, it was like they were already jumping ahead to wonder what they were going to wear to the funeral. Now that some time has passed what they say is, "You look great!" But it really translates to, "You look great for somebody who has . . ." I know what they're thinking. Few people say it, though. Margaret's father doesn't. He tells me, "I have a niece . . ." and I think he's saying "knees." I ask, "You had your knees operated on?" "No," he says, "I have a niece. A niece! She had that. She's fine." I say this is good. I know from Margaret that this niece—her cousin—had my same operation, then radiation. I also know from Margaret that in a while the cousin's cancer returned. So she wasn't really fine. I don't want this back. I worry about that. Already. I worry about a lot. I can feel the world resting on top of my skull and I can't shake it off. I worry that I worry too much. Or that I think about myself too much. Last night I told Tommy I just can't believe I have this, and when am I going to believe it? I was diagnosed in July and here we are with the furnace kicked on for the season, we're wearing sweaters, putting out the Halloween candy, and I still can't believe it. We sat with nothing but the nightlight brightening the dark and I told him I just can't believe it. He listens to me and it's such an enormous thing he's doing for me just by sitting there. I would be very tired of me by now.

"Cancer, cancer . . ." Margaret is sing-songing this after her parents leave. She tells me I've got better about saying the word. I know I have. I know I initially hadn't been comfortable sounding it out. I walked around the subject with language. But it's cancer. The word is the biggest thing.

≈≈

I'm trying to write some thank-you notes. Lots of people have gone out of their way for me since the summer, since this (look at me now, writing "this"—it's cancer). Since the cancer, lots of people have done things I need to thank them for. One kindness was a letter from Joan, who lived across the lake back when I lived in my A-frame on the lake. The first time I was served cold pasta—cold on purpose—was at a lunch with her and Jeannie, at Jeannie's house. It had broccoli in it and it was fantastic. Joan was diagnosed with breast cancer a couple of years back. She wrote to me even though we hadn't seen one another in ages. Again, I find disease an instant connector, or reconnector in this case. She tells me that the word is what's scary. The word. It does have a lot attached to it. A list of sick and dead people that goes as far back as your memory. "Full of cancer," my parents would say as they took off their coats upon returning home from somebody's wake. "They opened him up and he was full of cancer." I wasn't full of it, but it was in me. Doing its growing for however long, while I was unknowingly going along with my life, riding in the soldiers' convoy truck, happily rolling down the highway. A year ago on this day, I was in Chicago on a book tour, the weather was gorgeous for walking along the lake, everything was fine and fun, Tommy and I traveled by train and bus from there to Detroit and to Cleveland and to Buffalo and to home again, and on the final night I learned there was to be a second printing of the novel I was promoting. Reality then was a string of appreciated good.

This year at this time, it is the hospital every day. I walk into the waiting room and I look around and I think how everybody in here had their own moment of finding out they were sick. Their own second in which somebody told them they had cancer. Was it on the phone? In an office? Were they alone? With a friend, or a room full of family? What did they focus on as they heard the word? A face? The wall? Their hands? I looked at the back of a junk mail envelope on which I wrote the word as the woman gave it to me over the telephone that night. I always take notes of important phone conversations, a leftover habit from my reporting days. This time all I needed was to write nine letters: carcinoma. A word that looks as if it should be a town in California. I wrote CARCINOMA on the back of a junk mail envelope at the big table in my office. Standing, though I don't know what was holding me up because I don't remember my legs being there.

∽◠∽

I can't help but feel that I am doing this the wrong way. That I need to get over it already. I'm sick of reading all this Breast Cancer Awareness Month cheery stuff about how people are diagnosed with breast cancer and then a day after their surgery they're out campaigning for governor again. I'm not exaggerating—that was somebody's story. It's a whole lot more than two days after my surgery. It's October. And I'm still not back to resuming "normal activities." Or feeling anywhere like the normal I once knew. I still favor my left side. I still obsess. I still wonder what I did, still feel the guilt that I am responsible for this illness that has head-on-collisioned my life. Two days, my surgeon said. The guru says that was not a helpful thing for him to tell me right after my operation, and I thank her again. Everybody is different, Wendy says, timelines should not be slapped across everybody's recovery. And I agree. But I give the surgeon a little latitude. Doctors are busy. "I have to see twenty-two people today," one of them told me the September afternoon I went to Dana-Farber in Boston for the second opinion on my treatment. Those twenty-two people were what had prevented her from calling in sick and going to buy antiques at the Brimfield Flea Market that day, which is a big thing in the world of antiques and which was going on at the time in the next town over from mine, which is why she brought that up. I divide eight hours by twenty-two. She will be hopping. But she keeps me for an impressive amount of time, asking very detailed questions and going over the inches of me in the examination room, with Cindy sitting nearby and the wide-window view of more and more medical buildings, all of them surely full of people going through things they would rather not be going through.

As we waited for the appointment, Cindy and I wandered into the cafeteria, which appeared to have surprisingly good food for a hospital. But we wanted to treat ourselves later so we only got teas and ate sugar cookies from a bag Cindy had brought because, being a mother, she always has food along with her. It's her birthday today. It's also a month, exactly, from my surgery. I'm buying her birthday presents in the Dana-Farber gift shop. A backpack with teacups on it. A tray with two bunnies on the beach, on a blanket, looking at the ocean—Cindy and me in better times, little bunnies who don't deserve this shit.

After I am told that my second opinion matches my first one at the hospital back home, that the Boston doctors would give me the same course of treatment as the ones in Springfield, we celebrate with pizza the waitress serves along with a basket of bread, which is redundant but good. The hostess at our favorite Newbury Street café has seated us in the open doorway, as we'd requested. As we'd been seated on our last two visits here, one of them having been Cindy's birthday the year before, when our biggest concern was the selections on the menu. The weather today is perfect and blindingly sunny and we are there past any lunch rush, and off and on we cry, and drink wine, and once in a while we hug and it's low and very sweet at the same time.

# ❦ 27 ❦

Before I drive myself to the hospital, I drive to the Quabbin. I've loved the Quabbin since my earliest memory of it. In the 1930s, two decades before I came along, the state drowned four entire towns to make this enormous reservoir, mostly for the use of people at the opposite end of Massachusetts. There's that sad reality. But there's also the undeniable beauty of what's left, mountainous forest meeting water, all uninterrupted and quiet.

It's fall and to me the Quabbin looks the best in this season. But I'm too late for the height of the color. I was too tired to get here on time for that, too out of it, too uninterested. By the time I make my visit, weather and the season have done their damage to the leaves. Everything has a brownish cast. I climb to the top of the observation tower to take some photographs anyhow. That's another thing I've not been excited about recently. Usually I have a little spy-sized camera in my pocket, ready for anything. I save my photos in albums, draw from them, make cards and booklets with them, cut out heads to make badges and crowns on peoples' birthdays. Today I had to go looking for the camera, not sure where it was. It's with me here in the tower for right now, and up there with me are three people with thick Germanish accents, venturing how they have better-looking leaves at home, wherever that exactly is. The fourth guy, who must be their American host, waves toward the expanse of trees that runs all the way as far as you can see, to New Hampshire even, and he says, "To look at this you'd think nobody lived in Massachusetts." And he's right. For most of the vista there are no buildings, no fields, no farms, not much of anything. A town center is over there, Belchertown, and if you insert coins into the mechanical binoculars you can spot Amherst maybe, some smoke stacks, the defunct ski hill on Mt. Tom. But far and wide, there is nothing but trees.

Those people leave. Two women and a pack of little kids come up next. The kids are running and the women are yelling at them for the running. The noise of their thousands of stamping little feet echoes and drives me out. Down the stairs, on the fourth floor from the bottom, I spot a little bird flying up against the window. From the inside. Let me out let me out. It's small, like a chickadee, but is brown-and-white speckled, with a beak that's hooked at the very end. It raises its little wings up against the window glass, where you'd put your hands if there were somebody on the other side that you really wanted to see, like that cowboy man standing on the turnpike overpass clutching the chain-link fence. The little bird keeps still and quivers and reminds me of a bat, when you spot them out in the daylight and they're folded up and dazed and without an idea of what to do next. I easily put my hands around it. I have the bird in my grasp but it squirms loose and flies against the next window. Rests, with its wings up again. Get me out of here. From around my neck I take the beaded scarf Margaret bought me and I place it over the bird and gather it up and hold it away from myself so as not to shake it up more than is necessary. I feel bad for it, but if left in the tower it probably would go crazy trying to escape.

I take the stairs gingerly. A woman is coming up as I walk down. She looks at the odd bundle I'm holding out. She doesn't ask, but for some reason I feel I have to offer the information that I have a bird in here. I say, "I have a bird in here." She calls down to the man and the two teenage boys walking up behind her: "She has a bird, a bird in there." They don't know what she is talking about and I pass them without comment and three more floors down I'm outside, the bird is outside, we are outside, and I open the scarf and there is the bird, standing like a carving in a curio cabinet. Motionless. You can tell it's petrified. Its claws are dug into the fleecy scarf material. I loosen the left foot. It's like moving a piece of air. In an instant, the bird frees its other claw and flies away in undulating wavy motions like the shapes you draw to make sea swells, a peaking *W* pattern that takes it down the slope and above the brownish trees and across the road and far off to the northeast, over the great lovely wooded country that gives the sacred illusion that nobody lives here. I watch until I'm sure I can see it no longer, until it almost hurts to stare so hard, and I make sure that the dot that the bird is now is gone from here, safe again.

≈≈

"Friday," Carvella says when I enter the waiting room. And she starts laughing just from saying that. She's relatively new to the crowd, but not shy. She's always laughing. I want whatever they're giving Carvella. So I can be always laughing, too. I miss laughing, which once was a big part of my day. I miss lightness and naivete and motoring about my world throwing rose-petal wishes to everyone I pass. I want to be like laughing Carvella. But I haven't chatted with her enough to feel I can ask for her prescription.

"Friday," Annette tells me when I put my head in the dish. Though she doesn't need to say this. I know.

"I saved a bird today," I tell her.

And even though it's late afternoon and there are beds lined up in the hall like cars at the toll booths on Labor Day weekend, Annette stops her measuring and says "Really? Tell me."

# ~28~

Saturday again. People phone to check on me. They offer to drive me the upcoming week. Want a ride? Need a ride? I can drive, do you want me to drive?

Those who want to transport me to the hospital are those closest to me, plus some I hardly know. One woman I met when she was one of two people who attended a reading I did in Shrewsbury, and she'd claimed a chair only because she wanted a place to drink her latte. She e-mails me from out near Boston to say she wants to drive out here and take me to treatments. She is not some kind of freak, she just wants to help. Everybody wants to help. I'm blessed by that. But I'm lying here saying, don't help me.

Tommy goes into Springfield daily, but he no longer asks me to come along. He's heard over and again why I don't want the help: being driven to the hospital makes me feel like a patient. And other than an increasing level of exhaustion, I don't feel sick. I still don't look sick. I don't feel like a patient—like somebody who needs to be loaded into the passenger side and locked in and ferried to Springfield and back. They want to give me company. But I don't want the company. I want to get in my old blue Honda and turn up my tapes and focus on nothing but the road in front of me. In silence—no small talk, no intrusion on how I might be feeling that day, good or bad. I just want to do this myself.

It's control, Cindy says. She points out how illness that materializes out of nowhere makes you feel out of control—anything can happen, which is usually the case in life anyhow, but here it is, happening to you, in you. Your very body doing sneaky bad things. I reach for any semblance of control, of my time, my space, my life. Driving myself is one attempt. Walking is another. Writing, a third. I write this and I continue to crawl through the editing of the book that will be out next summer, when I'll tour for promotion, some nights reading to maybe just two people, while on others a couple of hundred might show up. Right now I can't imagine doing any of that kind of work, feeling totally unsocial right now, and able to look only at tonight, and maybe tomorrow morning. But next July? July is like another universe. Where will I be next July? Where will Molly Bish be? Today state police impounded a car in connection with her disappearance. Today eighteen members of the Central Massachusetts Search and Rescue Team combed a hundred and fifty acres in the Coy Hill Road area, and two hundred local residents gathered for the third vigil held since the disappearance five days short of four long months ago.

# ༈ 29 ༈

I get another saint today. Already, I know she is my favorite one.

Diane, who already has sent me the sorrier-looking Saint Peregrine, and who told me about not seeing the governor at the fair but seeing the ironing board, and the camels in the parade that did not make a sound, sent me this one as well. The saint is Agatha, noted on her card as "Patroness Against Breast Diseases." There is a saint for everything, I guess, and for everyone.

Agatha is quite good-looking for a saint, depicted here resembling a forties contract film star with crimped goldish tresses and a complexion of plain yogurt. The type who'd play the part of Shirley Temple's governess, lovely but stubborn enough to hold a grudge against the man who loves her and who must enlist the help of Shirley to win her back. To play the part of Patroness Against Breast Diseases, Agatha wears a long magenta skirt, and her white sleeveless top is what I guess must be bandages around her chest, but you could also see them as fashion in a New York boutique. She holds her left hand to her heart and her right one bears a frilly fern. There is a definite golden halo over her head.

Diane has written that she had purchased two of these cards though she can't remember where. Then she adds an asterisk, so if you go to the bottom of the page you find out that, "It just hit me: I bought these at the San Fernando Mission in July!" July. While I was waiting for the call from the doctor, maybe on the same day the nurse told me the news over the phone, Diane, whom I hardly know, was buying a saint card that she didn't know she'd send and that I didn't know I'd have occasion to receive. Diane also writes that she thinks Saint Agatha should also be the patroness of people with volcanoes in their back-yards, and she is correct because Saint Agatha is depicted in a yard with a slope behind it that leads to a big mountain streaming lava. I don't know if that's supposed to be a breast reference or what, but it's there. On the flipside of the card there is a prayer to God, who, it says there, showered heavenly gifts on the virgin Agatha. Help us to imitate her virtues during our earthly life, the prayer asks.

I go to find a saint book to learn what those virtues are. Turns out Agatha is not even listed. I wonder if she is an invention, someone cre-ated for these times of breast cancer awareness, one with a website and a line of gifts—ferns, volcano sculptures, sleeveless bandage tops—that are high-priced but nevertheless lure you with their promise of turning over an undisclosed percentage of profits to the American Cancer Society. I write that and I wonder if the times weren't always breast-cancer-filled and people just didn't know what was killing off their mothers and sisters and daughters and such. I met a woman who told me that so many women currently are being diagnosed with breast cancer because they are encouraged to go for exams: if they didn't go for the exams, there would not be such high numbers of people with the disease. I'm not making this up. But is Agatha made up? I will have to do further research. But even if she is fictitious, on this Sunday when I am just getting around to opening my mail from the previous week, I will take her as genuine and real.

# ❧ 30 ❧

My guru wonders why I wear the Walkman. She's asked this before. She says again how I could benefit from getting to know the others in the waiting room. She says they sometimes make such a din that the staff wonders what goes on in there. She says there's energy that maybe would help me and that sometimes solid friendships spring from the support found there. I say that this advice makes me feel as if I'm not playing nicely with the others. It's just that I would rather close my eyes and listen to the music. I would rather not get involved. I like to just get in and out. My guru says that's fine, she just wanted to remind me of what might help. And that's all she wants to do, after all, is help, so I thank her.

Though we had no huge connection, I do miss seeing Luz in the waiting room. Now I'm missing Annette in the lead-lined room. She is out again. Her husband broke his collarbone in a dirtbike accident and needs an operation and they are meeting with doctors. Today, as was the case the last time she was out, there are two people to replace her. Again, a man and a woman, though a different pair. The guy's name is Pat and he introduces himself as he passes me in the hall. "Hi, I'm Pat." His last name is Vadnais and I say I'll remember that because I used to follow the Boston Bruins and there used to be this Vadnais guy on the team, and the Pat guy says, yeah, Carl, and I say, yeah, Carl, but it's, like, ten hours later and I wake in the dark and I think to myself, no it wasn't Carl, it was Carol. Carol Vadnais. I should know that. I knew all that stuff then, in the early seventies, when I was mad for the Bruins. I read everything I could about the team. I collected the cards, saved for the magazines and the yearbooks, monopolized the titles owned by the library. I kept scrapbooks, one solely for columns by the *Boston Herald-American*'s D. Leo Monahan. I memorized the players' middle names, hometowns, their birthdays, and the names of their wives and kids and pets as well. I knew that Ken Hodge had a pool shaped like his number eight. That Derek Sanderson's father once kept a jar of stitches collected from his son's face and body during junior hockey days. I committed to memory career stats and could go head-to-head on Bruins trivia with any boy in the Bay State. Sure, that was a long time ago, but still, I knew well Carol Vadnais's name. My mind is muddy. I'm forgetting things. It feels odd because I normally have the recall of some space-age computer the CIA would store its records on. Cindy says there's too much going on with me to remember every little thing. Overload. Fatigue. I should give myself a break, she says, and I wish I knew how to do that.

≫≫

On my way out of the hospital, I see a woman sitting in a wheelchair just outside the wound care department, across from the ceramic wall-piece, the one in the brick hallway that I have finally figured out invites you to celebrate health and well-being. The woman wears a johnny and bathrobe and cold-looking slippers and is staring into the space that I pass through. Her arms end abruptly at the wrists, which are bound by bandages and do not lead to hands. A man standing behind her is brushing her long yellow hair in slow careful strokes and he is leaning in and asking her, is that OK? Is that OK?

Molly Bish's parents say they still buy too much milk, as they forget, for the second it takes to pick up another carton, that their daughter still isn't there to drink it. As for my friend Tim Kargol, he remains dead. And that woman in the hall, she will not get her hands back. Me, I walk to the parking lot in the soft fall air.

## 🦢 31 🦢

I find out what kind of bird I helped at the Quabbin tower last Friday.
I find my copy of *A Field Guide to Identification of the BIRDS of
North America*. The BIRDS word is in capitals like that, reinforcing
that birds are all you will find in here. I slowly turn each page trying to
learn the answer I seek. I'm thinking maybe the explanation, what type
of bird it was, might be meaningful. Like, this was a bird that landed
way off its track, was lost, separated from its flock—that would be
something to ponder. If it's a species you don't often see around here,
and if the book maybe would say it's good luck to spot one of these, I'd
take that. I'd take most anything even masquerading as a sign. I look
for the meaning of my strange new life every two inches of my day. In
the lyrics of bad songs I'd normally flip past on the radio dial. In the
lyrics of good songs on a tape that I pick up at random. In a look from
a gas station clerk. From a radiation oncology technician. In messages
on the signs outside convenience stores. In the AA slogans you'll find
written backwards in your rearview mirror when you spot the front
bumper of the eighteen-wheeler on your tail. JUST FOR TODAY, they say,
or EASY DOES IT.

I'm hoping the universe is sending me something easy to translate.
I need direction, guidance, and I need it spelled out on a wall in three-

foot-tall script, fluorescent orange spraypaint, with somebody standing in front of it waving a flag and pointing: here, here, this is why you're going through this, this is what will come of it. I want it explained to me, this is why the cancer happened and this is how you will fare, and these are the things your life now will hold. This is why you are acting the way you are, this is why others are as well. It's a lot to ask from a matchbook cover slogan, or a line on a T-shirt, a cookie fortune that says, "The hard times will begin to fade. Joy will take their place." Or from a little brown bird with a slope at the end of its beak. But in my normal life I am an optimist. And I guess some of that has spilled over into this hard time. If I have to have cancer, have it tip my life over as it has, I want some kind of prize at the end. Enlightenment, an answer to life's mystery, maybe a permanent feeling of placidity complete with the slightly stoned countenance that might accompany it. I'll go around smiling blithely with not a thing bothering me. Bounced checks, sudden deadlines, pepperoni on my pizza, I'll smile over it all, meet the problem with mindfulness, deal and go on. I want that, or something resembling it. I want the life equivalent of the case of Rice-A-Roni given as a parting gift to game show participants. I want to get something at the end of this. I'll wait and see.

～～

I go over each page in the BIRDS book. Several of the birds that somewhat resemble the little brown speckled one in the tower don't fly anywhere near New England. There is no mention that they might come even close, and no comment about the sight of them being a good omen or big luck charm. But—then—the real thing. On page 235. It's called a brown creeper. Not the best name, but it could be worse, as I see on the next page, where I find the pygmy nuthatch.

According to the book, the brown creeper is a common but inconspicuous small woodland bird and the stiff points on its long tail feathers are used as props as it works up and around a tree trunk. Its song is said to be high and faint, and rarely heard outside breeding grounds

"A single very high note" is the description of the sound I did not hear from it. These are short-legged small brown-backed birds that "creep" spirally up tree trunks searching for insects. Decurved is the word for the shape of the bill. The next and final sentence in the description is a single word: "Solitary."

I feel solitary these days, so I take something from that.

# ☙ 32 ❧

On my walk I pick up a piece of trash that turns out to be a wrinkled NASCAR magazine.

There are photos of race cars on the front, going around in ovals as they do. Moving so quickly they blur into a rainbow line, a painting with colors wet and running together. The cover is hyping a story titled "Proper Attire for Life in the Fast Lane." That is found on page 8, so I go there. They are selling a red jacket that reads BUD KING OF BEERS, and this will cost you $169. I figure out that the magazine is more like a catalog. Sponsor names printed on the wearables—Exide Batteries, Interstate Batteries, The Home Depot, Miller Lite, Dupont, Valvoline. "Wear the Winning Feeling," the page invites.

〰〰

A big white van comes up my driveway. It's a florist from the next town over.

He knows the way to the back door. He's been coming here often enough since August, three months now. I remember being slumped on the chaise lounge in the patio shortly after the surgery, and he was at the back door with some floral arrangement, saying to Tommy,

"Your wife's young, right? But she's sick?" I know some very good and generous people. Sending daisy-and-carnation arrangements. One time, an enormous fruit basket that had even kiwis and a coconut. I've yet to open the coconut, as it seems like a commitment. I await a special occasion. How many times do you have an actual real coconut?

This deliveryman has flowers, and he is at the foot of my back steps.

"Stella?"

I'm not Stella, I tell him. I think quickly how there's one across the street, an old one. Then I flash to the fact that she died a couple of years back. I'm not remembering. But once I do, the details float to the surface like air bubbles from the clam of memory that's holds them: how Stella's sister was an ex-nun, how they used to regularly dust the siding of their house with mops and yell at each other while doing that, with cursewords yet, and how Stella wore a net of a scarf over her big bee-hive hairdo all the time and warned me every time we talked not to get old, that I'd only get sick. Don't get old, don't get old.

"I'm not Stella."

The deliveryman points to the card, to the "Suzanne" written there.

"Stella," he reads.

"OK."

Then he goes, "Stella, you know, you been sick a long time," and I shrug and say, "I guess." I'm not going to start debating here.

"You don't look sick," he tells me, reinforcing what I think, and also underlining what my neighbor at the farm said when I returned her puppy after it followed me on my walk earlier that morning. "You look great," she told me enthusiastically, and I told her what had become my standard reply to such comments: "I would have gotten this ten years ago if I'd known all the compliments I would get." Her face fell and she hurried into, "No, no, no you don't, you don't wish that. . . ."

"You don't look sick," the deliveryman says again. Then he leans in and asks quietly, like somebody else might be eavesdropping, "Whatya got?"

I squint up my eyes and lean into the other half of the space between us and without skipping a beat I tell him, "Cancer."

He leans back, looks me up and down—for what I don't know—and he says, "You don't look like you have cancer."

"But I do."

He considers this, tilts his head. "Che-mo-therapy?"

"Radiation."

"Well, you look good. If you didn't have a husband, you'd go off with me, right?"

"Oh, you're right."

Because I've given the correct answer, I am handed what he was there to deliver, a basket with a handle and fallish-colored flowers that smell like Sunday afternoon company.

At the hospital, I'm happy to see Annette back at work. Her husband remains in great pain due to his collarbone being knocked out of place and disks bulging in his neck. He thinks the front brake of his dirtbike locked up as he was zooming along. He doesn't remember, but thinks that's what sent him flying. You usually don't remember the last moments of something like that, only the waking up and knowing, better than you know anything, that something bad has occurred. Annette looks tired and a little older, if it is possible to get that way in a matter of days. I think I'm looking older these days, but I have a hard time looking at myself in the mirror anyway. The whole of me I can take a look at. My face, no. Cindy told me she couldn't look in the mirror for a year after she got sick. And this is with clothing on. Again, even though that is sad to learn, this is the type of information I am grateful for, to know that I can have these thoughts, and that someone has had them before me.

After the treatment, Annette changes the subject of how she is to how I am. It's started off as a good day for me, an unusually positive feeling cloaking me, I'm feeling lighter and brighter and considerably out of the fog that had been reaching for me. Tommy is better, though still remarking about his own experience at every chance, and because of that often finding, as I have, instant kinship in others who have been down the same medical hallway. I tell Annette, "Well, I feel better today, actually. I haven't felt well in my mind for, like, a month and a half." She clarifies, she meant to ask how is my disposition. So I say, "Well, I've been kinda down. . . ."

Annette's eyes get very big. "I didn't know this! Every day you're in here and I didn't know this?"

"Well, isn't everybody who comes in here . . . aren't they all depressed . . . or is it just me?"

Annette gives me the big eyes. "Well," she starts, "lots of people have a hard time here—gee, oh, I didn't know—why didn't you tell me?"

Her empathy and concern perhaps should further brighten me. Instead, they whack me back down to zero. I'm in the mud again. She's walking me down the hall, her hand on my shoulder. I tell Annette that I indeed was fine when I arrived here today, now I feel awful. She says I can feel free to cry. I know that. I cry about three time a day, like something written out on a prescription form by my general practitioner as he ignores his phone calls and concentrates on what instrument I should try to play, his son plays the flute, did I know that, it's good for you to do something like that. I cry like I used to eat before I lost my appetite, and that was frequently. Today I've been feeling well. I haven't cried at all. Now, suddenly, it's all I want to do.

"Go ahead," Annette tells me and I squeak out that if I start, I'll never stop, and that is something genuine in my soul and not just a line you might hear a character say in a stupid movie because how could you actually cry forever? But that is what I feel I could do. Annette makes the sound "Awww" and she leads me into an examination room and shuts the door behind us, then she hugs me as I sob into the crisp shoulder of her white lab coat. She is small, feels birdlike, brown-creeperish even, which is how I felt about my cherished downstairs grandmother the many times I hugged her. I worry I'm going to break Annette in two, but I lean on her anyhow and sob and, when I can, I whisper that I feel bad. Even now, as I write this, I'm coming back to that pain. I feel bad. Annette says it's coming to the hospital every day that renews it all. She sees this in patients. Every day, over and over, no break, a constant reminder that you are sick. You have this, you have this, a bad mantra hammered home. Annette gets what I'm feeling and I'm grateful. Annette understands what this is about and that is a blessing. As if on the cue of my thinking that word, she tells me there is a chaplain in the department. "I'll give you her number. And you can have my home number. You can call me anytime."

She's telling me all this and I'm looking at her through the blur of my tears and I'm asking, "Doesn't it make you sad to work here?" Annette answers, no, she likes the job. Oh, there's the odd mental-health day off she must take as a respite, you need that, but, mostly she sees the nicest people here. "When I was a bartender, I saw people crying because they didn't have enough money for another beer. I'd say, 'Hey, you don't have any problems.'" She doesn't work in a bar anymore. She just works here. With people like me. Past the end of her shift, she is in an office hugging a stranger. Telling her it's going to be OK. Saying the stranger can call her. Anytime. Anytime.

I am given a yellow stickum on which Annette has written the name of the radiation oncology chaplain, whose work it is to deal with people like me. She also writes down her own home number so I can call and interrupt her husband from his pain and from their own life problems.

"Call me," she says. "It's OK."

# ❦ 33 ❦

On my walk I spot something in the stubble of the cut hay. At first, I think it's a foil wrapping from a cemetery arrangement. You get that out here in the wide field, things that weather has knocked down, blown around, carried from the intended gravesite to another down the row. Courtesy of the weather, a woman who never left the village in which she was born gets a flag that signifies she was a veteran of an overseas conflict. A stone unvisited for years sprouts a tangled bounty of someone else's pots of plastic roses. A childless man lies cold beneath a Styrofoam cutout reading MOTHER.

But what I see in the field this morning is obviously not for the surely dead. It is a flattened balloon reading GET WELL. There is a cartoon drawing of a bear on it, lying in bed with a thermometer in its mouth. The balloon is tied to a long purple ribbon. I walk it to the blue trash bucket next to the water spigot and deposit it there.

Before my appointment, I help Margaret, whose neck is bothering her badly and who stands and instructs as I clean a closet holding her ex-husband's stuff way in the back, behind rows of her daughter's clothes and toys and a purple inflatable chair. Two boxes of brand-new shoes, two big cartons of clothing, that's what is harvested. That, and the real find—a box of his old pot-smoking and related drug paraphernalia. Margaret says she could score points with the neighborhood kids using this. I'm just thinking I could score, period. Since I started telling people about my cancer, more than a few have come forward to offer their services procuring pot should I need it to ease queasiness from chemotherapy. And when I tell them I will not be having chemotherapy, they are genuinely disappointed.

The boxes of shoes and clothes are heavy and I carry them down the stairs and onto the porch, and Margaret will place a call to Larry so he can come over and pick them up. The box of pot-smoking stuff goes in the trash bag that I take away to my bin at home. Another bag is set aside for the Goodwill. I help Margaret put new sheets on the bed, something she cannot do without pain. She changes clothes while I clean off her dresser. There is laundry, books, paperwork, things thrown there in the overwhelm of her disability and her sadness. I find myself working without knowing I am working. For me, this does something. I clear everything off right down to the wood, where I find some jewelry boxes, and a huge Bible. I dust those, attempt to put the Bible on the adjacent bookshelf, but that's a mess as well.

"Tomorrow," I say, "I'll do the bookcase."

"Next day," Margaret says, "The world."

∽∾

Annette has brought me a plant. An ivy, in a pot wrapped with the kind of green foil I often find out in the cemetery rotary. A white ribbon sticks from the soil. I'm given this when I enter the treatment room and remove my blue sweatshirt.

"I wanted to do something for you," she tells me. And she embraces me. There are good people in this world—that is what I'm thinking.

I am told the radiation oncologist wants to see me. I didn't have an appointment, so this is unexpected and gets me worried. Dr. Mary Ann starts out by saying she has been thinking about this for a week, thinking as she goes home about just what she wants to say to me, and she doesn't know where to start. You don't want a doctor telling you this, that something has concerned her to the degree that you are filling up her head for days and even on her off time. And then, suddenly, this is how my mind works, I'm thinking, oh no, she's going to ask me why I wear my Walkman while I'm in the waiting room, why don't I play nice with the other girls and the odd boy? But she doesn't mention that at all. What she says is, I'm in a gray area. I might benefit from another week of radiation. High-dose. Another week added to my visits here. She want me to think about it. But I don't want to think about it, because she already did and I trust her. My feeling is, I'm coming here already, and as much as I'd like to finish, it's not as if I've been counting the days, so what would be a few more added to the total that I don't keep track of anyway? I say, "Fine," and I ask her about her writing, which she likes to do and wants to do more of but has yet to find the time for.

# ❧ 34 ❧

Back to Margaret's bedroom. I straighten the bookcase, the debris on her sewing machine, a decorative wicker shelf on which there's a jar of junk including Larry's old driver's license. I arrange the closet. She points out the clothes she wants to donate. I take away three bags, plus two of trash. At that moment I realize that, the afternoon before, I'd mistakenly put the Goodwill stuff in my trash bin at home, and brought the trash bag to the Goodwill—the trash bag containing Larry's pot. Margaret thinks this is priceless, but also a lost opportunity: "We should have waited and thrown his driver's license in with it."

I replace a wedding photo in the hall with a picture of their three children. And I wonder what the three notice these days when they come home from school. Things are changing around them. In the family structure, and in what they see hanging on their walls. Somebody tells me it's a good thing that I go to Margaret's. What I tell them is, it's easier to arrange and fix up somebody else's life than it is to do the same in your own. I'm organizing her room and I want the afternoon to go on and on, I do not want to have to leave. I want to stay there tidying. There's something to it that has nothing to do with anything else going on in my story, and that is very welcome.

October still crawls. It is the end of the fifth week of treatments but it feels like five months. Some people are treated for months—over a period of months—so things could be worse. And some people don't have one of their dearest friends free at the same time, home twenty-four hours a day for months on end, sitting still as possible with injured disks and the new reality of single motherhood, the very same months in which you are passing her house daily and she is idling there in need of company. I look for the meaning of this, Margaret and I being off work at the same time, having these life-smacking things happening to us simultaneously. I think of this while seated in her easy chair, on the borrowed electric massage cushion with the clicker that allows you to control which part of you should get the vibrating, exactly how much jostling should go on, and the precise amount of heat you would like to feel beneath you. I press the button for the entire body massage and everything around me appears to jiggle earthquakishly.

I tell Annette about this cushion, that they should have one on the machine. But she says not even a pillow is allowed. Only the plastic dish, that is your sole luxury. I have the routine down now. Head in the dish, Walkman and its wires above that. The ocean song cued up and starting just as the machine begins its whoosh.

Once I'm home, I spot Susan sneaking into my garden with a plant. It is a thyme. I open the window and ask her if she has the thyme. Corny, but she likes it. We have not visited for a while. She says through the screen that she misses me and there is a pulling sincerity to her words. So next, there we are in the kitchen for tea and gift cookies, pizelles fried up by my cousin Gen. Seven years ago, Susan had a tumor in her uterus, then a hysterectomy, then awful thoughts. It wasn't cancer, but she got her share of fright waiting to learn if it was. She says how it's difficult for people to understand how something like this, something this scary, can affect you. What I'm learning is, everybody who gets sick deals in their own way. "Everybody expects you to go running to your mother or your best friend around the corner. That is not what happens," Susan says. "Maybe for some, but not for anybody I know." She says people you wouldn't have or couldn't have predicted can end up being the ones who help the best, whom you rush to, cling to. You want to run far from everything you know. Susan? During her storm she looked in the classifieds, had a strong urge to suddenly move, looked wistfully at this little purple cottage on the way to Northampton and thought how nice it would be to be there alone and doing her paintings. Me? I keep seeing the ocean as the pull. Living where I could see it daily, hear it, visit it, stand in it, inhale it, stick my face in it year-round. I have no idea what this means except maybe that I am headed in some new direction.

≈≈

I get an e-mail from a cousin who believes that, through my silence and keeping to myself, I am neglecting my mother and other relatives who worry about me. It is well-meaning, I'm sure, but it angers me. Nobody seems to get it, that I want to and have to think of myself now. That I shouldn't be spending my energy worrying if someone feels left out. I am learning things from this experience, and this is one of them: everybody has a process, and they should be allowed the freedom to find out what it is.

With perfect timing, another tape appears in the mail, a package from Ireland holding a cassette of a British man recorded in Boston reading the poetry of a woman from Provincetown. And this man says that Mary Oliver says:

> You do not have to be good.
> You do not have to walk on your knees
> for a hundred miles through the desert, repenting.

You only have to let the soft animal of your body
        love what it loves.
Tell me about despair, yours, and I will tell you mine.
Meanwhile the world goes on.
Meanwhile the sun and the clear pebbles of the rain
are moving across the landscapes,
over the prairies and the deep trees,
the mountains and the rivers.
Meanwhile the wild geese, high in the clean blue air,
are heading home again.
Whoever you are, no matter how lonely,
the world offers itself to your imagination,
calls to you like the wild geese, harsh and exciting—
over and over announcing your place
in the family of things.

There are no commandments in this country I'm now finding my way around, and trying to find my place in. I'm making them up as I go along. And if they turn out to be unpopular, what can I do? It is my life. That is another thing that dealing with cancer is giving me—the billboard-high message as visible and blazing as Mr. Bigda's HOPE, the reminder that this is my life.

# ≈ 35 ≈

Cindy phones. She does this every day. She says I called her every day
when she was in my situation. Though she doesn't actually use a stupid
word like "situation." She uses "cancer." Anyhow, I don't remember
making so many phone calls to her at that time. I do remember some,
and Cindy often sounding terrible on the other end and my not
knowing what to say because what do you say to these people? I do
remember bringing her silly presents like ankle socks with goofy pat-
terns, and also plants that I also should have offered to put in the
ground for her because now when people bring me plants I have no energy to put them in the ground. I do remember driving her kids to a
few obligations, the son home from band practice and the daughters to
and from a writing class they were taking at the library. Before they
went to all that I helped them with dinner. We had sweet potatoes and
I can't remember what else. Things about that time are sketchy in
my head. Sitting for hours with her David in the waiting room
of the town hospital, making small talk and trying to concentrate on
some book, and then they are saying Cindy is coming up from surgery,
and she's in the hall now flatted to a bed and she's groggy and looking
very tiny and sunken into the mattress and there are tubes from her

everywhere and I don't know what to say then, either—this is my best friend, she should not be there in this state. I told her I was glad things were over for her, and that I had to get to work. Which was not a lie. Back then I was assigned to three small towns on a 2 P.M. to 10 P.M. shift. I left David and Cindy alone, as they should be, and then I was starting my car in the parking lot of the hospital where I was born and where my father died, and where the tests were done that told me a month earlier that I had a suspicious cyst that turned out to be nothing bad at all. I drove away. Untouched by anything bad that day, as I had been a month earlier. I went to my office and then out to cover a Board of Water Commissioners meeting at which they discussed next year upping the price for the water that is tanked and sold to residents who wish to fill their swimming pools. I can remember that, the place, the little gray building in which the commissioners met, the exact basement room where the meeting took place, how it was cold despite being the end of the summer, how the ceiling pipes were exposed and I thought it was the perfect place, plumbingwise, for a bunch of water guys to meet. I can remember all that from the day on which Cindy had her mastectomy. But I can't remember phoning her every day. Not that much. But she doesn't lie, so I must have.

When she calls me today, a long Saturday, I laze on the couch in the headiness of knowing that October is almost history. We talk about a woman we've met, a very ill woman who recently told us she feels bad she cannot meet all her obligations. She was supposed to baby-sit but canceled and went to the mall with a friend instead, and worried all the while that she would be spotted by somebody who knew the baby's mother, and that person surely would go back and report the sighting, and the lie. She has breast cancer. The outlook is poor to the point that she's started to give away her savings, just so she can see people enjoying these gifts while she's still around. She is nearing the end of her life, and she is feeling bad about enjoying a day doing what she really wanted.

Cindy listened thoughtfully to this story. Then she asked the woman this:

"What's it gonna take?"

The woman thought for a second, and after just that second, was astounded. You could see the rays of light suddenly beaming from her brainspace. She'd never considered her life in this manner. She felt empowered. Licensed. Grateful. If having a cancer that numbers your days can't allow you an afternoon wandering around a mall, what would?

On a better day, even with my good prognosis, I can feel the same way. I can actually see this as my Rice-A-Roni game-show parting gift —the license to do and say what I want, not just what others expect of me. It's a most important prize, and I would like to walk away with it.

# ❧ 36 ❧

Daylight savings Sunday. Clock change. Spring ahead, fall backward.

Sue is driving out from Provincetown to visit me.

She's wanted to visit since the surgery. We finally worked it out, and I look down the road and await her and her love and humor.

We met eighteen years ago, when she was in need of a place to live, and I was in need of a tenant to help with the mortgage on the A-frame. She was a writer with a talent that still makes me envious, and also is wickedly funny and a great cook, and she came into my home and life with a large selection of fashionable clothing and accessories she encouraged me to borrow. While we both went off to work at the newspaper, her Irish setter, Amos, guarded the house from his place on her bed, while my shepherd-cross, Roxy, watched from mine.

My bed is now taken up by now-house-dog, Leo, and, over on the Cape, Sue's is warmed by Louie, a similarly Brillo-paddish-looking piece of love on four legs. Today we will walk the dogs and catch up on the news. Once they get here—it's the first snow of the season and they're delayed in that. This gives me time to think about the day, which is an odd one for me, the annual Rays of Hope walk in Springfield, a huge fundraiser for local breast cancer programs. A lot of what I've had or benefited from in this health adventure was paid for by Rays of Hope grants. Machines, staff training, even the CD player in the needle localization room I was in last June, where I crushed the hand of the Rays of Hope–trained volunteer who stood next to me for comfort as a radiologist snaked into my left breast a thin wire that would help the surgeon find his mark.

So I'm more than all for fundraisers and such. But when Christine called to say she wanted to put together a team to walk, I just couldn't get into it. It's strange to suddenly have a medical problem that people want to raise money for. I didn't want to attend the walk. Too many people, too close to reality right now. Then a woman who once was my baby-sitter phones to say she wants to put together a team as well. Will I come along? I can't go to the walk. I don't want to go.

Sue and Louie finally arrive, snow swirling around their Jeep. It's Halloween time and they've brought me a toy bear dressed in a moose costume, and also a bag of candies shaped like sets of fangs. I have nothing for them. So we go to the grocery and stock up on the makings of a big salad of the type Sue ate once in Paris and she tells me about the twenty-five-year-old Bedouin who is e-mailing her since her trip to Jordan, in the guise of trying out his English. She now is a freelance writer and literally travels the world. She is what I consider brave, both in the stories she reports and in the way she lives. She has moved on from a difficult youth and young adulthood, and bears the wisdom you can gain along the way from that, if you are so inclined. As she was.

Because I can talk to Sue about anything, I tell her the stupid things people have been saying to me, their takes on diagnoses, their making light of something that is very dark to me, their horror stories and their pitting their illness against mine: "If you had your pick of cancers, you'd want breast cancer," one woman told me. Sue says, "Oy," and then wonders about it all: "Why does everybody have to put their big fat two cents in? Whatever happened to saying 'I'm sorry about your problem and I'll be thinking of you?' They have to recommend a book or give you the phone number of a friend or tell you their tale of woe, on and on."

I love that. What she said, and how she put it into four little lines. Why indeed does everybody have to put their big fat two cents in? If I have learned anything so far, it is to withhold mine. Let people be with the reality of their situation. Sue talks about Frank, her dear friend who died of AIDS. She was one of five friends who divided his ashes and she once took me to the place where she placed the portion she was given, a scrub-pined dune with a view of the airport and the sea beyond. I had heard about Frank forever, but had never met him. This dune was as close as I'd ever been to him in real life, so I touched the sand right there.

Sue said that when Frank got sick it was all he could think of, he dwelled on it, in it, wanted to spell it out, say it. He had the idea he was going to write on every bill he got "I have AIDS." Sue told him she was going to do that, too. "Only, I told him I was going to write on my bills 'Frank has AIDS.'" She's told me lots of Frank stories. She knows a lot of people who have had sorrow. The diseases are different, but the result is the same: terror, and a scramble for any shred of the world's understanding.

We eat the Parisian salad and the fang candies. We laugh a lot. Tommy, upstairs writing, thinks we sound pajama-party. I open the futon for Sue, Louie jumps on, Leo tries as well. For fun, we watch something very scary, the Wolfman on TV. Lon Chaney, the real thing.

# ❧ 37 ❧

Margaret, Sue, and I go out for breakfast. We all once worked together at the paper. Now Margaret is the only one of us left there, reporting on business when she is not home with a bad neck and a new divorce. Actually, Margaret is the one who introduced Sue to me. I was reeling from Rosemary's death. Sue had just been hired. Margaret learned a bit about her and said, "Go and introduce yourself. She's nice. She has a dead friend, too." So I did. I went over and said something like, "Hi, Margaret told me you have a dead friend. I have one, too." We went to lunch at a place that specialized in broccoli soup. We talked about our dead friends. We soon became a pair of living ones.

It's been a while since Margaret and Sue have seen each other. I listen as they catch up. There is something good and warm about sitting back and observing the back-and-forth of old friends. In preparation for my upcoming dairyless existence, I order an omelet that is ninety percent cheese with about a teaspoon of egg thrown in. We have the waitress take our photo in the booth. Then, outside, we get Margaret's camera from her car and go across the street to the auto body shop to find someone to snap an outdoor shot, which a man does as we stand in front of a sign that warns you that if you leave your car there overnight, any damage or loss will be your liability, not the auto body's. A the stranger figures out what button to push, I wonder how I will look in this photograph. Do I look sick?

It is difficult to see Sue leave. We hug for a long time at the Jeep parked outside an optician's, dozens of pairs of fashionable designer frames watching us from the display window. She heads back to the Cape. Margaret goes off to her physical therapist appointment. I drive down the street to the hospital. An earlier visit today, to meet the new machine that will give me my prescribed final week, the big technical term for which is "boost."

Once inside, I realize that in the commotion of getting myself and Sue and Louie out the door I forgot my blue sweatshirt, my charms, the angel, the card, the rock, the picture. I've left the Walkman in the car as well. Is there a meaning to this going in without my armor and my diversions? Did I do this intentionally and not realize, to show myself I need only me me me? Who knows.

In my regular treatment room, the radio is off. After the machine whooshes, there is no noise at all. Just my breathing. I don't like that. Then, I'm back in the waiting room for ten minutes or so of having to really listen to what is around me, the pages for the doctors and nurses and for assistance in a treatment room, shorthand: "Nancy to Cobalt." Because it is a different time of day, I see no jolly Carvella, no white-wigged woman. The room contains only me, and a young couple to my right. The woman says "Excuse me, how long do things take?" I think how this is a good question. About life in general. And, if she means about radiation, I certainly look like the person to ask, seated here in my johnny, freezing without my sweatshirt. People don't come in off the street wearing johnnies. I am one of "them," and I am being asked the lay of the land. A member of the senior class giving a confused freshman directions to the gym. I tell this woman that a treatment will take her less than ten minutes, and she corrects me that it's not for her, it's for her father, he went in there a while ago, shouldn't he be back by now? She is holding her man's hand tightly and she is worried and is looking at me with the same kind of big eyes I probably am giving people day in an day out, only hers are circled with black liner that she has not even attempted to blend into a more natural look. She wants to help her father. I want to help her. She is not saying, "Don't help me," so I go ahead and do. I tell her what I know. That this will not hurt. He won't feel anything. That the staff is very nice and everything is well-timed and they make it as easy on you as they can. I become a spokesperson for radiation oncology. I could be on an infocommercial somewhere: if you have cancer, I have the place for you! I am selling what the woman wants to buy. A solid recommendation, a believable testimonial. I see her face ease, a little nervous smile starts, she nods and twirls her rings. I don't say this to her, but I put myself in her place and find it a painful fit. I loved my father like the moon and I would not want to be the daughter bringing him to this place day in and out. I do tell her her father will be out any second and that everything will be OK, I'm sure, which is a slip because I don't like to.say that type of thing anymore to anybody, even a woman who would appreciate a nice lie.

A technician appears in the door and I am directed to a new room. This is the home of the linear accelerator, which will do the final week on me. To get there, you must walk down a little corridor with a radiation-danger sign greeting you, then Disney posters lining the walls, and stars stuck to the ceiling, and I realize the sad fact that children must come in here, though I've never seen a single one pass through the doors of this department. The nurse escorts me around a corner to the left and says I can sit on the table until the doctor comes along. I don't have my sweatshirt and I'm freezing. The only thing I remembered to bring was a book, some poetry by Reynolds Price, whose work I admired long before I found out that he is in a wheelchair due to spinal cancer and that he wrote "Turn," in which he compares his radiation experience to "twenty-seven daily trips to Hiroshima."

What I know about poetry could fit in the period at the end of this sentence. But I know what I like, what is speaking to me. I sit and go over the Reynolds Price pages while there on the table. Above me a mobile of Winnie-the-Pooh characters hangs without a movement

the sad Eeyore being too much for me to acknowledge. I look elsewhere around this new room. Its machine is huge, takes up about a
third of the space. It's more modern-looking than my previous one, a
rounder design, newer looking plastic-and-metal body. And the room
is different—busier, with a sink and bright white cabinets as if this were
a kitchen you'd be inviting your family and friends into for a nice evening of cooking and dining and relaxing. Along the other wall is a huge
computer screen, burning brightly with a chart of all the appointments
of the day. My name is on there, highlighted in black. According to this
screen, I'm in for "marking up." I read the other names. It's none of my
business, but I do. Another old-reporter souvenir. The patients repre-
sent a sprinkling of nationalities. Another Disney theme: it's a small
world, after all, when you scoop a net of cancer folks and get a wide
smattering of the globe: Puerto Rican, Irish, Polish, French, Italian,
Asian, English. Across the line from the names are the parts the machine will aim at on each person: breast, breast, breast, breast, lung,
breast, scalp. Breast.

The nurse comes around the corner as I'm reading the names and
the problems. She tells me I'm cold, which I know, and she fetches me
a heated blanket, which is one of the few things I've come to like about
the hospital situation—heated blankets. I wrap it tightly around me. In
the black machine dial my reflection looks back at me beneath the Pooh
characters. A surprisingly dressed Dr. Mary Ann enters, jack-o-lantern
earrings swinging, witches and brooms on her jacket. I never would
have taken her for somebody who would wear fun clothes, but there
she is, in them.

I'm told to lie down. I'm given a real pillow, rather than a hard dish
for my head, and the technicians say this is the only machine on which
you are able to use a pillow. The table is elevated with a whirring noise
and the doctor instructs the technicians: "Linear with a kick," which
I don't ask the translation of but which sounds like a dance. Nobody
does one, though. Instead, a couple of the women go to work moving
the machine. It's dark in the room now and they're measuring various

points on my breast, from the tattoos in and out and around and the nose of the machine is coming very close to the left of me as the doctor is making more dots on my skin and I start to get nervous, which surprises me, and then I look up and see Annette and her Christmas curls there on my right, she is there as she promised she would be and I want to reach up to her but have been told not to move. She hasn't deserted me in this new room. She is there, with the others. Annette says, "It'll come very close but it won't touch you," and the nurse is saying she has to move me, and she does and I don't help. I get positioned and the doctor is finished doing her calculating and the group of them are making some sort of decision and then one is asking me if I am allergic to tape. They're drawing on me and they're sticking tape on me and taking another half-naked picture for my files and then, like that, I'm done.

I get lost on the way out, I don't know where I am in this new side of the hall. I bump into Annette, who takes my arm and leads me past the gurneys of patients waiting with big thick files stacked on their midsections, and I am back in the familiar hall. I find my cubicle and my shirt and coat. I remove the gown and see the big lines of purple beneath the tape. They tell me this type of ink will wash off in time. But I'll still know it was there.

That night, I read the newspaper account of the sixth annual Rays of Hope walk. The participants, all seven thousand walkers and three hundred volunteers, got snowed on at the same time yesterday that Sue and I and Louie and Leo were getting snowed on and walking the woods to the river, and Louie got lost for a time and we yelled for him frantically because he is a bit deaf and if he wandered off would he know how to get back to us? I don't know how far we all went that day, maybe four miles. Most of the walkers in the benefit completed up to five miles, and they all combined to raise $588,000. Over the six years, the effort has raised more than $1.2 million, which is something. Volunteer Leslie King is quoted as saying, "I feel I have something to contribute to those who are now going through this [That would be me]. The secret I've found is having positive thoughts. If you rely on negative thoughts, that's what you get in return." Another woman said she raised funds for all those women who have died from breast cancer, and all the women currently fighting it.

"And I do it for myself," she added, "hoping that if I ever get diagnosed with it, there will be a cure."

⧼⧽

Another big sum was in the news today—an anonymous donor from the Springfield area pledged $60,000 to the Molly Bish reward fund. Six thousand tips reported so far to police, and tests on the impounded white car still ongoing.

# ❦ 38 ❦

In the locker room, the woman with the bushy white wig arrives wearing a Halloween sweatshirt. There is a haunted house on it, a Victorian building with cartoony ghosts flying in and out the windows. I tell her I like its colors. She tells me it's handpainted and I ask if it holds up in the wash. She says, "Well, I only wear it once a year. So it should last for twenty." As she has worse things than colorfastness to worry about, I'm hoping she can enjoy it for at least that long.

Halloween. October 31. The long-awaited end of the month that felt like a year. A holiday celebrated by the wearing of costumes. People dressing as someone other than who they are. Slipping into another skin. Even for a day, that doesn't sound too bad right now. My mother has an attic full of costumes she's made for parties over the years—a Christmas tree strung with working colored lights, a padded golden mummy in a box with a cutout for your face, a flounder designed so you walk sideways and look flattened out. She and my father used to attend polka weekends, which are just what they sound like, polka-ing Friday to Sunday and all other kinds of mayhem going on, including a costume party. I could have borrowed one of hers today. But I'm in the same old costume: johnny, blue sweatshirt with jammed pockets, earphones on.

Back in the waiting room, I wait for my guru appointment. The TV is turned to the soaps. *General Hospital,* which I guess makes sense for this waiting room. Today's story of course revolves around a big costume party. The women seated next to me exclaim how the actress now running the café on the program used to be on *The Young and The Restless,* just last week it seems. Why do they jump shows, the women ask me? I say that's probably because this is the soap that receives all the awards—wouldn't they all want to be on the show that gets the awards? The women answer yes, yes, of course, they certainly would if they were actresses, that has to be it.

On this show that gets all the awards, each actor is wearing the kind of costume you'd rent at great expense—elaborate royalty and Dracula and Elvis—and there's fake fog and big spidery decorations in the background, castle walls, dark organ music and howling sound effects. I have brought the candy fangs with me to give out for trick-or-treatment. I'm called for my appointment and at the same time there comes a news break on the TV. The dour female announcer reads that at six they'll have the details on the woman who faked cancer in order to scam people out of money. I stop in my tracks. The women next to me silence their talk about the café actress, who they think is way too thin, like most everybody else in the cast. The others in the outer waiting room look up at the screen. I can feel the energy churning in those chairs. I want to say something out loud, like let's go and kill her, a big group of real-cancer people banging on her door with clubs from the caveman costume one of the people in *General Hospital* is wearing. But I am a pacifist, even when sick, and now angered. I walk off to see the guru.

# ❧ 39 ❧

It is November, and I enthusiastically turn the page.

On my calendar, October's picture is a familiar scene—a photograph of the Berkshire hills at the other end of my state, which looks like my part of the state, only a little bit taller. Appropriately, November's illustration looks like a good party. Five parrots. Blue and yellow. On the branches of a leafy sunny tree. This is a calendar sent to me by The Nature Conservancy. They want to save the last "great places," areas of rare beauty and tender ecology that remain untouched by human intrusion, and they sent this seeking a donation that would allow them to do that, to buy up parcels of land. I like this organization. I see open space disappearing with disconcerting regularity, some of it right down my street. The calendar tells me these birds are macaws and they are found from eastern Panama to southeastern Brazil, two places that are not right down my street but that I still care about. They are threatened by illegal hunting and habitat loss throughout their range. If that doesn't get you concerned, the page says there are a whopping twelve hundred other bird species whose futures are dark. In the photograph, the macaws don't appear to be rattled about this fact. They seem to have a peace about them. They will feel the weight of their problems another day, perhaps. But not while this picture is being taken.

Beneath the macaws are all the blocks that make up the month. Thirty of them. Some have been preprinted by the calendarmaker due to their importance: Election Day, Full Moon, Veterans Day, Thanksgiving. Others bear my scribbles: town taxes are due today, the first. Mary arrives from Ireland tomorrow, the second, Johnny and Christine will be married on the fourth, and on the sixth I should put out the recycling and then go off to see the guru. On the seventh, trash day. On the eighth, this might all be over with.

For the first time since I flipped to this page two months before to roughly calculate the radiation stretch, I see the long blue lines I have run through all the blocks up to the eighth. After that I have written, "end?" just like that, with a question mark. I don't say end of what. I still don't know if that day will be the end of the treatments, but it gives me some form of an idea and, turning the page again just now, I finally become interested in the number I have left. This might be over with on the eighth. I can see that, I can handle that. I know that once I am put on the new machine, I will have a week left to go.

≈≈

In the newspaper I spot this: "Fake Cancer Victim Sentenced."

She was from South Boston. Age twenty-five. Pretended she had ovarian cancer and got people to give her a total of $43,000. Got a two-year probation sentence after pleading guilty to larceny. Was ordered to make restitution to her victims, to perform three hundred hours of community service, and to stay at home between the hours of 8 P.M. and 6 A.M., something I can't imagine would have an effect on her disease-faking scamming behavior. She used the money for cosmetic surgery, a new car and weekends in luxury hotels. I've had enough surgery to suit me, thanks, but a new car would be nice and a weekend away very welcome. But I don't have the $43,000 to fund any of that.

The woman's lawyer said his client is remorseful, but has been advised not to make a public apology. For legal reasons.

Radiation oncology is very busy. People in hospital beds are lined up along the walls like planes ready for takeoff. Annette has told me several times how this complicates things—it's lots of work accommodating both the outpatients and ones who have been admitted to the hospital. I anticipate a wait. I play the songs for a lead-lined room. The ocean one, its rocks clacking in the surf. Across from me sit two women and two men. Two pairs of patients and drivers. The men are talking about how good everyone at work has been since the news, how understanding. The younger man, who has to be the driver, is reading the radiation booklet that everybody in here gets handed. He holds it up high and in front of his face. He either needs that position to see clearly, or he doesn't want to look across at me and the others in our gowns, reading our *In Style* magazines or staring at our shoes. The pair of women are joking about the route they took today, was it shorter or longer than the usual one? (Longer turns out to be what they decide.) The woman who is the patient is wearing a baseball cap. She is next to the TV set that is only for educational and instructional videos. If you want to be educated or instructed you must ask a staff member to run the thing for you. I've yet to see anybody watching one of these. In the main waiting room the TV plays constantly, loud, the regular channels. News about people faking cancer and news about there being no news from Warren, except a heartsickening aside that still circles my head: Molly's clothes still find their way into the family wash.

# ≈ 40 ≈

When I started radiation, the summer Olympics were being beamed from Australia. Athletes swimming and playing basketball and throwing all types of balls and spears. Faster, farther, stronger, longer. The big events for which they'd waited most of their lives. The announcers looked tired and far away and neither they nor the viewers, none of us seemed to know the actual day on which the games being shown had been played.

It's nearly winter now. I'm on a health marathon that has taken me from spring to summer to fall and now into the end of the year almost, and I am ready to hibernate. I sleep thirteen hours a night, plus an afternoon nap. The first-thing walk isn't as easy as it used to be. For starters, it's tougher to get out of bed. I go to sleep at eight like a grade-schooler. I'm still tired when I wake at approximately the next time the clock reads that number. I stay under the covers, looking out the window at the big pines and the valley of blue space they create in the sky. The wild geese fly through that space, in, then out, calling to me, as harsh and exciting as the Oliver poem in three dimensions. I don't know if they have their own poem, but crows are winging past as well. And one small bird this particular morning, moving through the space, then out and gone like the mindfulness that has been recommended to me as a sanity-saving measure—observing a thought you have, watching it in your mind and then letting it pass so the next one can come along. Being aware of each moment and not letting it get its claws in and rule you. I find it hard to do but I'm willing to try. I lie there and watch the birds and geese come and go, and hear Tommy getting his cereal or snapping on the computer and I wonder when I'm going to sit up and put on the walking clothes and go. I've always been out before the schoolkids waiting for their bus. Today, by the time I get on my walk, they probably will be having lunch.

I get a phone call from somebody who's pretty much kept away from me. One of the people I should know better than to tell my true feelings to, but when she asks, I think maybe it's a sign, maybe here is my opportunity this morning to say, I'm so glad this all will be over soon, to voice that.

"But it's not like you had chemotherapy," she butts in. "Now that would be something to complain about."

≋ ≋

Out of the blue, Annette tells me my final treatment will be today.

Today.

"Last day in here" is how she puts it, and I go, "Huh?" and she says, "It's the last day on the cobalt machine." That's it? Friday I start on the new machine. Simple as that. I don't know what to think. I am happy, sure, but there's a sense of something ending, and I can hear the voices of more than a few former cancer patients I've met along the way who said they were jealous of me, explaining that I was lucky, that I was still doing something active, still undergoing visible treatment, still working daily at something that was supposed to make me better. They were done, sent on their way to live with the hope that they had taken the right course and everything had worked and they were healthy. I finally had the number I hadn't wanted: five more treatments to go. Five more trips to Hiroshima and I'm done.

Thursday. It is my last trip to the cobalt. And it is unceremonious.

Put the head in the dish, get shifted, I don't help. It is all the same as it's been. Except that today I did see for the first time the light way way up in the nose of the machine that lowers down toward you. The table was in a different position and the thing was over my face when I first climbed on. I looked up into it, curious. A clean, bright, white light was looking back, peering through the cavern, bits of dust floating lazily, as there is dust even way up in a hospital machine. I don't think the light was any kind of a message. Just a light. And I was seeing it for the first and, I hoped, the last time.

# ≋ 41 ≋

If she loses two more pounds, Peggy will get a tattoo.

She tells me this in the Olive Garden, where we are meeting for lunch. I've known Peggy since the first year of high school, and she shared an apartment with Rosemary while she was doing her master's at MIT. Shawn is our waiter, and he's the cliché-chatty type that, after he asks how are you and you say fine how are you, he answers I couldn't be better to tell you the truth thank you! All with big smile and while fanning out the oversized menus.

Peggy would like a dolphin tattoo. She plans to move to Florida soon. It will be perfect, for sure. Me, I don't know—I would have liked a design rather than a thing. Maybe a swirly circle, a meaning-laden yin-yang. What I got was a plain dot, and then another.

Shawn has overheard Peggy and he informs us he already has a tattoo and he hikes up his left pant leg and there on his calf is a guitar. I ask him what kind? It's a Strat. He loves guitars. He says he was in a band named Suckerpunch. I ask what kind of music did Suckerpunch play? He considers me and then says, "Nothing you'd like," and I ask him how old do you think I am and he doesn't answer, just grins, and there goes his tip. I don't care how old I look, that's not the problem— I just don't like Shawn's attitude. Anyhow, the question is moot, he' with Suckerpunch no more. Going to computer school instead. And has a girlfriend. "You can't do those things and be in a band," he informs us.

Peggy wept with me on the phone the night I called her about the diagnosis, and came over for tea a couple of days later. The teapot leaked on the table and, though not because of that, we cried again. Today we don't cry. Just eat. It's enjoyable enough. I have the house-special endless bowl of house salad with the grated cheese on top. Plenty of it.

❦

In the waiting room this Friday there's a new family, an old Puerto Rican lady, who is seventy-six and is being treated for lung cancer. And her daughter and granddaughter. The grandmother is adorable and tiny enough to carry around in a tote bag. She smiles at everybody and speaks in the only language she knows.

The granddaughter, about eighteen, is sweet to her grandmother, but when the Spanish starts, she feels she has to apologize. She'll roll her eyes and she'll tell you, please excuse her grandmother. "She speaks Spanish to everybody."

❦

The new machine sounds like my refrigerator when it finally bumps up against the wall and makes its vibrating noise until you give it a good shove and then it's quiet for maybe another couple of weeks. The nose of the new machine comes in very close to me when the technicians guide it. Then Dr. Mary Ann appears from somewhere and asks can she take a look at my electrons and even though I again don't know what she's talking about I answer, why not, everybody else has.

On the ceiling there is a cutout for some sort of electronic box with two red lights that resemble eyes. Beneath that is a screw that makes the nose. Then a beige wire that curls like a mouth. It's a smiley face looking down on me here in the new room with the new machine. It's saying four more days four more days. From nerves I start to babble and I tell the doctor and the technicians about the refrigerator noise and then I show them the face in the ceiling and they say when you are in a room all the time you do not notice things. They look at it and they laugh about it. They are giddy. It is Friday afternoon and their work is almost done for the week. The machine draws even closer to me and everyone leaves the room. It makes that refrigerator noise, and then there is silence.

# ❦ 42 ❦

It's the day of Johnny and Christine's wedding. I drive myself. Not because I don't want to feel like a sick person, but because Tommy is
an usher and left the house early, in a tux, looking very good even
if neither he nor I could figure out how to put the decorative fake
mother-of-pearl covers on the buttons of his shirt. I wear all black, then
my big red winter coat even though it's going to be in the seventies.
These days I'm cold no matter how warm it gets.

I arrive at the church and my in-laws are seated in a limousine
parked out front, something you don't see every day as they are not
limo types. Mary and Kathy, Tommy's two sisters, are there with them,
the door is open and they are all waving me to crawl inside. It's the kind
of vehicle you see on award shows, or rented by high school prom-
goers. Extremely long and with a bar and glasses and napkins and ste-
reo and VCR and moon roof and seating for maybe fifteen people. The
windows are tinted so you can't see in, but you can see out perfectly.
We do running commentary on everybody who walks by: he looks
terrible! She's gorgeous—look at her! Who's that? Nuns? Dressed like
hat?

Finally inside the big church, I sit behind my nephew Riley, who is
ive and who spends the ceremony spitting into an empty TicTac case

and then tipping the box, fixated by the saliva rolling around inside. His mother ignores him because what he is doing is keeping him quiet. Christine comes down the aisle to the piece I am learning to play on my visits to Margaret in a slow duet on her piano, octaves apart. Pachelbel's "Canon." I follow it with my fingers. Christine has a parent on each side of her. She looks ready to cry, and also like a picturebook princess.

Her brother is a priest and performs the ceremony, and also delivers a lengthy customized homily that gets everybody laughing at a few points. I'm freezing in my winter coat and in the scarf for capturing birds. Women walk up to communion in sleeveless dresses and I'm outfitted for the North Pole. Before the reception, I remove the coat when we line up for family photos. Our backdrop is a gazebo on a common of a recreated old New England town. All the buildings surrounding the green were moved here decades ago to create a history museum. The setting is pretty, the sun is full and warm and the fall leaves cascade as if someone is up there in the tree releasing them at perfectly timed intervals. Everybody looks fantastic. But I feel miles from it all. A strange removal that for months has been like a nagging cough that you forget after a while is not normal. Some people ask me how I am. I don't know if they're asking me just to ask, as you would of anybody, or are they asking because they know something. I answer OK, which covers both. I always used to say good, fine, even if I wasn't. Since the diagnosis, I hear myself always answering OK. Two women inquire, and they plow on to say that a relation of theirs just had a horrible time with her treatment. So they know. So I ask "Radiation?" No, it was chemotherapy. "I hear you're just doing radiation." This is what people say.

≈≈

All the couples are invited to the dance floor. The idea is to find the pair that has been together the longest. The music starts. Some sort of waltz. Tommy and I are not good at traditional dances. We can jump around well enough, but this sort of thing isn't that. In preparation for our wedding, we took lessons at an Arthur Murray Studio, which I still can't believe. You look at your life sometimes and you say, "I did that?" And this was not even an orgy or anything. Just dance lessons. And I still can't believe that was me there. But it was me back in early 1984, and that was Tommy, too, taking advantage of another six-weeks-for-twenty-five-dollars deal, shuffling around a shiny wooden floor and not really understanding what we were supposed to be doing. But we wanted to look good for our first dance at the reception. And we did, once we stood still.

There's been no improvement since, and on the day of Johnny and Christine's wedding we scrape around in a circle as the disc jockey asks everyone who's been married for five years or less to leave. Then ten years or less. We make it up to the twenty-years-or-less mark, and stand aside to see who'll be the last ones left. The honor goes to Christine's parents, in whose kitchen I helped apply the LOVE stamps that delivered the invitations that let everybody know about this big day. The Tatros, who have been together half a century, get their names announced by the d.j. Everyone applauds. Cameras flash. Johnny and Christine join them in the dancing, the newest members of the club moving to the same beat as those who've been in it the longest. The parents can dance well, like most people's parents I know. They look happy at this moment, a big pleasant island to which they've swum, making it this far through the waters of regular everyday life and past the hulks of rotten tragedies, including the sudden death of a treasured son. Everybody has stuff. I look at the Tatros dancing there in their finery and I think this again. Nobody is spared. Dance while you can, I guess, whether or not you know the steps. It's OK to make them up as you go along.

# ❦ 43 ❧

I lead Leo out the back door to load her into the car for a drive to the deep woods. She yanks my arm from its socket as she supersonics herself toward the flock of wild turkeys parading through the backyard. With big loud round gobbles the turkeys fly—and they are not very good at this, Volkswagen Beetles taking to the air—or they run and shuffle into the woods, beyond her reach, a stray one escaping this way or that. There are about thirty of them and they are beautiful, gray-blue, hefty and mysterious. Cool things to see. It is November— do they know about Thanksgiving? If so, do they worry?

I am worried about everything. I should just worry about myself. That is what Cindy suggests as she and Leo and I walk through the Sportsmen's Club property, which is our destination this morning. She talks again about control. She says illness is a time when you want control over everything you can control—decisions, for example— because cancer is a thing that makes you feel out of control. It just happens, and often, as is my case, you don't know why and the doctors don't know why—it just happens. So you feel if cancer can happen to you, anything bad can happen—why bother to lock your doors or drive safely or turn away dairy foods? Things can happen. This also makes you want control over medical decisions and how you live your life. Say, if you just want to be off by yourself, as has been my case. That is important. I feel confused and ask Cindy how long did she feel that way and she says what I already know—everybody is different. She was confused after her cancer and she is confused now, eight years later. She says everything that happens to you from now on will reflect back on the experience, will have something to do with the cancer. She knows this as fact, but she can't and doesn't know how long I will feel confused.

"You can't say, 'Well, how did Cindy do this,' because that's how Cindy dealt with cancer," she tells me. "And you will do it differently. Two hundred people will do it two hundred different ways, because they are individuals. You can ask for ideas, but ultimately you will do it as you alone do it."

We can walk safely in the woods on Sunday because there is no hunting allowed on that day of the week. No one else is taking advantage of this fact. We follow a trail we've never been on, around a boggy area. Leo ventures into the muck and gets even blacker. At the edge of a pond we spot four big trees, maybe eighteen inches across, felled by beavers, neat and in a row like pencils on the first day of school. The beavers also have begun to chew the trees into measured sections. We try to imagine them working there all night, if that is when they do this sort of thing. There's the trail they take to their pond, the little slope they must use to get their logs into the water. Later on we come across another beaver pond, this one marked by an information sign that tells us, among other facts, that beavers are vegetarians, which, Cindy and I know, will reduce their risk of breast cancer.

≈≈

In the afternoon, Tommy reads a big stack of newspapers and I sleep like my ancestors on Sunday afternoons gone by. We always had a big Sunday dinner in my growing-up years, and after the meal my grandfather and father and uncles would go into the living room and turn on the ballgame and then sleep while the women cleared the table and put away the leftovers and did the dishes. I would wipe because I've always hated putting my hands in greasy water. I never once heard any of those men apologize for sleeping while the others were working. I now sleep just as they did, without apology, and deeply, in the middle of a Sunday afternoon.

## ❦ 44 ❦

I wake to more noise from the geese. I consider skipping the walk. This is one of the days I actually feel sick. Today, if anyone asked how I was feeling, I would use the word and say I feel like a sick person. Fittingly for a Monday, I'm draggy, very tired, also burned. Half of the front of me looks like it's been to Aruba and was exposed to the sun for a week, a red and peeling and blistering mess. The other breast looks like a "before" shot. Pale and flawless and innocent of anything that's been happening just inches away from it daily at 3:30 P.M.

I dress and get going on the walk. At the cemetery, beside the circle waiting for its chapel, there is a small sedan with nobody inside. I make my usual laps around the circle, then continue to the edge of the woods. I know this must be the car of a hunter, and on the way back I see him emerging from the trees, setting some big dark lump onto the field. He's already put down a quiver of arrows. He has a fluorescent orange peaked cap on, and a camouflage vest. I wonder why would you choose both those things, and not one or the other, decide to be concealed, and scream out that you are there? He looks at me and I turn and I abbreviate my usual route. I don't want to see what he has killed. My peripheral vision tells me he has returned to the woods and is bringing out another victim. I don't want to know.

On the way to the hospital I'm bothered by something in this bad novel I've been given. The main character, who had breast cancer a couple of years back, is advising a friend who's just been diagnosed that she should make a list of things that her friends can do for her. They will want to do things. It'll make them feel better, says the survivor. And I wonder why now, at the worst time of somebody's life, should the woman in shock be thinking about finding a pen and a piece of paper and making a list of stuff so other people can feel better. Other people. Other people. What about her? What about me? I know it sounds whiney, but it seems ridiculous to me to go to that effort of worrying about others when the others are totally capable of feeling better if they want to.

I rant about this, in the car, aloud, alone. I usually don't talk out loud to myself, but today I do. I verbally join myself in the anger and it's a good bit of snarling that I get out. I go to Margaret's and I rant some more. She consoles me with frozen Almond Joys left over from Halloween. We have tea. Her neck is bad today. I vacuum for her because that will help her. She has no list of things that would help her, but I know about her being unable to vacuum, and I am someone who wants to help. I don't vacuum my own house these days—Tommy runs the machine and is astounded by how you could almost build a new dog from all the hair collected. But Margaret's house I can manage. Because it's smaller, and because I want to help.

In the waiting room, I sit next to Carvella and her jolly-ness, and across from the two older women, the one with the wig and the one who is always accompanied by the man in mud-spattered pants. The appointments are running about forty minutes late. Everybody's pretty quiet and into their own worlds, reading or listening to their own versions of songs. The ocean. The big sky. A world away from here. And then

Carvella pipes up to remind us that election day is tomorrow and we should vote before we come in because there is no guarantee we will get out of here on time to do that. They all start in then. Carvella, displaying a bit of waiting room negativity, says that whomever we vote for he'll be a liar, a president can't get anything done alone, he has to kiss up to and buy the help he needs, and if the others in government don't like him, they'll squash him or they'll kill him. The two women across from us nod that she is right. "That Hillary is a smart girl," the man offers. "A smart cookie." Then all of them go on about Hillary's Bill, what a stellar job he has done. I don't add a word. Just turn up the volume.

Two technicians I don't know are running the machine. I take my place on the table and the first one asks me, "Could you move?" In a couple of seconds I answer, "You mean me?" And she says, "Yeah." I think how in all this time I haven't once been asked to move. For a more than a month it was don't help me, and now these people want me to move. Where's Annette, who doesn't make me do a thing except even on my lousiest day smile at her true goodness? I don't spot her in this dark room. Just the two new women doing their measuring and moving. I worry that maybe Annette's husband isn't doing well. I ask about him, and her, but nobody in the room knows anything, except that I should move. Now.

≫≪

As much as I look forward to seeing my guru, I have forgotten that today is my final visit with her. I knew I had an appointment, but thought it was tomorrow. Nothing is really straight in my mind. So, suddenly, without forethought or preparation or the thank-you gift I was still mulling, I am sitting in the tiny room with the couple of chairs, just she and I, no Holly around, talking about what the end of treatment might be like. I would love to install Wendy in my home. A nice corner room, maybe throw out the dining room furniture and make her a little apartment there, keep her for whenever I had something to deal with. But I can't do that—I can't even make further appointments. Due to the overwhelming demand for the services of radiation oncology, Wendy can do no more than assist patients while they are patients. Once treatment is over, you are on your own, out in the world to either depend on your own smarts once again, or to hope you can find another guru with half as much insight as the one you were assigned to. There are too many patients, too few Wendys. And that's a pity on both sides of the fence.

I have just this last fifty minutes or so. She and I talk about what the end of treatment means to me. I tell her I know the last day is Thursday, three days away, but that I'm not really spreading the word, because I'm fearful people will do kind things like bake cakes or come to my house with congratulatory banners, and I'll have to throw things at them. Those are the kind of people I know, the type that populate my circle and have done their best to love me at a time when I have not been that adorable. Plus, I don't want to borrow trouble, because I really don't feel my experience is over. I tell her what Cindy said, that a lot of the process is just about to begin. Now I'll have the time and increased energy to figure out what I want after the cancer. The guru nods and agrees. I'll have to tell this fact to Cindy, that as one of her last official acts as my guru, Wendy agreed with her yet again.

# ❦ 45 ❦

I throw myself out the door for the walk. The hunter's car is on the circle again. I do my laps past it and see that in his car cupholder he has a Dunkin' Donuts coffee, and on the back window ledge has three big arrows. The feathers are day-glo so he can spot them after he shoots. Next lap around I stop and look at the points. They are smooth and round, not the stabby triangular Native American-artifact shapes you might imagine. I think of the deer in the woods, the ones I see often, going about their deer lives, normal activity, maybe thinking (if deer indeed think like this), hey, I have it made, being a deer isn't half bad. And then THOCK there is an arrow sticking into the neck. Out of nowhere. No idea where it came from. Life changed in an instant.

It's election day. Bush vs. Gore. I drive to the polls. One of the ballot questions is whether the state's two dog tracks should be closed in the interest of ethical treatment of animals. A supporter of the question stands at Four Corners with his pet greyhound in a coat even though the weather is warm. I pull into the town hall parking lot just behind a man and a woman I know. I used to see the wife and the first thing I'd think of was her breast cancer and the second thing I'd think was, she's probably gonna die. It is in your mind like that. One thing, then the next. Some people you look at and automatically a description pops up in your brain every single time: "young widow"; "my high school lab partner"; "tireless volunteer when she could be enjoying her retirement years on the couch"; "said he didn't know why but he just didn't love me anymore"; "owns the farm where I once saw a cow being born"; "taught me how to use a checking account"; "holds her husband's hand on the way into church but actually hates him"; "opened his door and said 'why don't you trick-or-treat in your own neighborhood,' knew us even though we were wearing masks"; "uses the men's room at the gas station because he's too cheap to pay for town water"; "was in a prisoner-of-war camp"; "got arrested last year for growing pot in plastic kiddie pools hidden up in his attic"; "idiot"; "nicest person in the world"; "pain in the ass."

This woman, who for several years now has formed the words "breast cancer—gonna die" in my mind when I spotted her somewhere, has had a terrible time with her disease, and it is truly something that she remains alive and is here on this election day, getting out of her car to go and vote for a new president. I try to gather some of the trash on the floor of my car to kill time until she and her husband go inside the hall. I just don't want to talk to her, nice as she is. I just can't. Something about the prospect of speaking to her frightens me. Trouble is, I don't have that much time to waste—I'm voting just before I go to the hospital. And I've promised to stop by Margaret's. So I have to follow them sooner or later. I watch them walk up the stairs, past the town hall staffers' sweet seasonal display of pumpkins. She and her husband, in their late fifties or so, wearing matching coats like those you'd put on twins. I wonder if that was intentional, or is that just something that happens after the years, you start looking alike, you start wearing some type of uniform.

We're all inside now, and I'm walking way behind them as they complain how the polling room has been changed and where is it now? And where are the ladies who always sell pies on this day for some cause? They follow the signs to the polls, no sign of pies anywhere, follow the signs, they check in, I check in, they go to their booths, I go to mine, and with the pen provided I mark the little circles, first for Nader, then Kennedy, then to say the dog racing should be made illegal because I like to place myself in someone else's boots so I think that if I were a dog I would not want that life. I go to unregister, which is what you must do after you've checked all the boxes you wanted to, and next to the registrar people is a police officer who was in my high school class and back then was so small the boys used to stuff him into his locker and twist the combination to keep him in there. He says hi, I say hi. It's busy, he tells me, and I nod that it appears to be, and then Mr. Skaza, who always mans the ballot box, shows me how to put my ballot in the new ballot box and, as always, I check what number voter I am. They've phased out the old-fashioned box, which had a crank on it and when Mr. Skaza turned it, a bell would ring and a new number would roll into view like the odometer on your car when you progress another mile. This newfangled machine sucks in the paper like the shredders people are buying for home use to keep all their ultra-secret information ultra-secret, and the number changes on a little digital readout. It tells me I'm 534.

In front of me, the couple I'd hoped to avoid is stalled and chatting with the police officer, the guy telling him he must like to sit there because there are all those nice young ladies there to keep him company. The police officers says ahah. Then the man turns and greets me. His wife does, too. Because it's what you so often say automatically, it falls out of me, the question of how she is, and she answers as we walk toward the door, "Going along, you have to keep going along, right?" I answer yes, you do. In this small town where most people know what's going on with most of the other people, I don't know what she knows about me. And it really doesn't matter. I just don't want to get into it. Especially with someone who "really has it," as is this woman's case, and is my worst fears walking and talking alongside me. We leave the building and we're noticing the pumpkins there and the weather here and then her husband says goodbye and veers off toward their car and the wife does the same and I'm relieved, but then she turns abruptly and walks back to me and goes, "I have to say this to you," and I'm there waiting for the big cancer advice or insight or whatever she can give. I'm thinking you've been through everything, tell me what you know, tell me what you want to say to me. Tell me what I should be doing or thinking. She does. She fixes her stare and tells me, "What gets me is those people who say they're undecided. I mean, they just don't know—and here it is election day. They had them in the paper this morning. Photos of these people and below them it said 'Undecided.' How can they be undecided? These campaigns have been going on for years. They say they don't have enough information? What more would they need?"

Of course it was not what I expected, so I start to ramble, I answer what shoots to my mind first, that it's like those people who have a baby and you ask what's the name and they say they haven't decided yet. Like they didn't have any warning this was going to happen. They had most of nine months to think, or at least come up with some contenders. "It's kinda like that," I tell her. "How much time do people need?" and she says, "I don't know," and shakes her head in disgust. Her husband has pulled the car up so she gets in and they wave and drive away, in their coats, past the greyhound in his own.

Margaret is antsy about having to be out of work for another month. But she needs the rest. The extra month at home wasn't her idea—it was her doctor's. He feels going back now would erase all the progress she's made. One more month would really help. She and I talk about how work can define you to a degree, can create a hole when you enjoy it and then are without it. Even as I recount that, at home this afternoon, I realize it. I put down a letter, a word, a sentence, and I've created something. And creating is a need I've had since forever, nurtured in my home by an artistic mother and by a father who could have built the White House from a box of matches. Crayons and paper were always left out for our use, and however young my sister and I were, we were invited to sit by my mother at her sewing machine or stovetop, by my father at his cellar workbench or backyard garden. And no matter how crooked the straight seam or bent the nail, we received praise for what we attempted, and encouragement to do more. Making stuff has been so much of my life, such a source of fulfillment. Certainly, the books I now write, something I'd really never dreamed would be one of my accomplishments, but little things, too, starting ages ago. Sitting on Mrs. Bigda's basement stairs, a first grader in the 4-H Club, trying to coax a skinny yellow headband from a slippery skein of yellow acrylic yarn and two seemingly mile-long needles. Bookmarks from hairclips, vases from bottles, necklaces from elbow macaroni. On to music, drawings, paintings, photographs, pottery, a mural that covered the side of a building, a wood-and-chickenwire-and-papier-mâché high school mascot panther so large its legs had to be sawed off in order to take it from the auditorium to the big game. More photos. More paintings. More stories. Then lots of stories. In the newspaper, the nonfiction of real life, delivered daily to your door. Then, in time, fictional ones I tried to make sound true, available at your local bookstore or library. All resulting in the same wash of quiet satisfaction, that this came from me. And if I don't do anything else today I've done this, made something with my head and hands. I tell Margaret that I couldn't imagine not doing this writing every day. So I can feel some measure of the hard time she must be having, without the work that has been so much a part of her life for twenty years, especially at a time when so much else has dropped from her day. She tells me she'd like more of a pep talk—would I come with her as she goes to her polling place in the basement of the big brick Protestant church down the street?

I accompany her not only there, but right into the booth and I help her make the choices. She votes for Nader, for Kennedy, she votes for the registrar of deeds and her reason for that is that he kisses her every time he sees her, exactly the type of behavior that lost him my vote an hour earlier. She votes against the dog racing without my prodding or having to give her the dog's-eye view of the issue. On the way out, one of the officials confuses Margaret with someone else and says she thought she was a Libertarian. I say no, but she's a vegetarian, and the woman says OK. We take another route home, past city workers trimming trees and outright cutting down ones that you can see are surprisingly rotten to the core when they are felled but from the outside look as fine as any of the others. Then we head past the old-age apartments where my easygoing aunt, Cioci Nellie, lived after selling her house, then right by that actual house on East Street. I remember Sunday visits spent in there, me spilling orange soda on her carpet more than a few times and her never yelling at me for that and her being the kind of aunt, and adult, I way back then thought I'd like to be—somebody who doesn't make a big deal out of nothing. I tell Margaret about the Polish Christmas Eve *wigilias* held in the big finished cellar of Cioci Nellie and Uncle Joe's house, Mary Ann and me seated at the kids' table and being young enough to be awed by my cousin Stevie running his finger through the candle flame. I look at the garage with its overhang for a patio and can see the parties out there, the last one being after the funeral for Uncle Joe—which turned out to be such a reunion that even years later when relatives spoke of it they'd say, "That was at the wedding—oops, I mean the funeral. . . ." It was that enjoyable. Margaret says sometimes funeral parties are the best.

≋≋

At the hospital there is a huge wait. Beds are lining the hallways again. In one of them, a very old man has four family members clustered around him, all of them looking very worried. They regard me with their concern as I pass and I give a half smile. I place a stack of my old magazines in the waiting room next to Carvella, who is happy for the new material. I take my seat in there and the chairs are almost all taken. The woman with the white wig, a newer chemo woman, the little Puerto Rican lady and her daughter and granddaughter, one older man, a younger man. I have the Walkman and the songs and I'm listening to that with my eyes closed, doing my breathing and removing myself from the talk. Next to me the chemo woman is looking over the shoulder of a kid who is flipping through a fashion magazine and both make their commentaries about the clothes. I open my eyes to that and see the room is now even more jammed, and anybody who is a companion of a patient is now standing, all the chairs occupied by those of us in hospital johnnies. I want to joke that if anybody else wants a seat, they should get a johnnie. Or cancer. But I don't. I stay with the music and the back of my eyelids. Forty-five minutes later, I get my time on the linear accelerator and the technician is asking me do I want to put my arm up and would I move to the right and there is no Annette to do it for me and make me feel cared for.

There are only two more treatments after today's. With this one, for the first time, and though I know it is impossible, I can feel the rays when the machine starts its refrigerator noise. I feel the way people early on were imagining I would, as I'd first imagined, too—that I am being cooked, or at least preheated. When it shuts off and the nose is moved away, I peer up into the machine's passageway.

"What's in there?" I ask the technician, and she laughs at my nosiness and says, "The thing that directs the beam or whatever." That doesn't help me to know more, but I say OK. I look into the machine and down the long tunnel of metal, and, just like the other one, there is the clean, clear light at the end.

At home, I stay up the latest I have in two months, watching the election returns. There is to be no answer tonight. It is history-making. People are saying everyone will remember this election year.

# ~ 46 ~

I finally find something on Saint Agatha of the cancer prayer card. In *The Penguin Dictionary of Saints.*

This dictionary admits it is not sure, so bear that in mind, but it thinks she existed in the third century. There is a question mark after that information, to show the uncertainty. It does say there definitely was a virgin martyr named Agatha at Cantania in Sicily, who was venerated "from early times." How much earlier than the third century can you get? They don't say. Nothing more is known about her.

"Her worthless legend [yes, they do use that adjective], of which there are many versions, tells us that she was a girl of noble family who was pursued by a man of consular rank, named Quintian. When she rejected him he proceeded against her as a Christian. Having been handed over to a woman who tried in vain to corrupt her, Agatha was tortured in various ways, and we are told that at one point Saint Peter appeared in a vision and healed her hurts. But eventually she died from her sufferings."

Among the barbarities to which Saint Agatha was said to have been subjected was the cutting off of her breasts, and the dictionary says she is often represented in artwork carrying them on a dish. With curious consequences: the resemblance of the shape of breasts to the shape of bells led to the adoption of Agatha as patron saint of bell-ringers. And their resemblance to loaves, something I never really thought of but that is what the book says, apparently accounts for the ceremony, in some parts of the world, of blessing bread in church on Saint Agatha's feast day, February 5.

On a plate. The morning of my surgery, I had the needle localization to determine the exact site of the tumor, and then a procedure in which radioactive liquid was shot into my lymph nodes and a machine traced its journey. I got wheelchaired around to these appointments with a stack of files and X rays on my lap, and on top of that sat a lidded plastic container the size that you'd have filled with half a pound of cole slaw from your local deli. It had my name written across the top, and nothing inside until they later got inside me. At least my container had a lid. Agatha was walking around with her breasts on a plate. My prayer card holds no mention of this, just shows that 1940s starlet version of her and her fancy fashion top, which I now know more about the reason for.

≈≈≈

There is no result yet from the election It is too close and things in Florida have been crazy, with the count there still taking place. Everything is delayed. But it doesn't stop anything in my life. I take the walk. The hunter's car is not there. I am happy he is gone. I have the circles and the field to myself, the creatures have their woods back. As I walk hear snappings way down in the trees. Something is in there, and I et it be, give it a morning off from fear.

At the hospital, Carvella is laughing again. The staff like to remove he johnnies from the dressing room just before she arrives, and leave sign reading NOTHING FOR CARVELLA. She'd phoned them earlier to sk how many hours late were they going to be today and they told her ne'd better bring her supper. That made her laugh some more. She ughs about everything. She confides that she is getting burned on er neck from this, and that she is feeling poorly, but you would never know that if she didn't say it. I tell her she has a good disposition whatever is going on, is that all the time or are you just bringing it out for this? I do not feel I have been a good patient. It would be nice to be sitting here laughing and joking with the staff and phoning ahead to have more fun. But I just can't. This whole thing has shaken me. Carvella laughs again, no surprise. She tells me she works down at the unemployment office. "There are hard people in there every day," she explains, "giving you a hard time. The only way to be is to have a laugh about it. Otherwise, you would not be able to go in there day after day."

Carvella goes back to reading her Prince William issue of *People;* he's celebrating another birthday, which I think took place back in the summer. A technician comes to get me, a nice one named Linda, and Carvella makes a fuss that I get to go in first. The Linda person is in a good mood, too, but I haven't seen her act otherwise. She knows I have the one day left after this.

"One day left, Suzanne, one day." Linda keeps using my first name in every sentence she speaks. Angela at the front desk without fail calls me Miss Shea every time I crack open the door to the department. "Good afternoon, Miss Shea." I wonder how they can remember the names, there are so many people coming and going, so many people with something wrong.

# ❦ 47 ❦

I walk, but it's an effort. I'm tired on this last day of the treatments. And weepy. And rushed and crazy. I'm to have lunch with a friend, an overdue thing I've canceled maybe four times. Then I'll get to the hospital.

The friend had studied to be a nurse. Gave that up to get married. But still loves to talk medical. Her litany since the summer, the few times she's been in touch, has been this: there is really nothing wrong with me. As she puts it, "You really don't have it." It's not Stage Four, I'm not in a coma, so it doesn't count. Maybe there should be the big red blinking lights from the treatment room going off in my head, telling me this is not a good thing to do, meeting with this person on the last day. And maybe there are lights and I just don't see them. So I go.

We're talking and soon she's asking me how the course of treatment is going. She talks like that, medically. Course of treatment.

"Well, the last one is today."

"Thank God!" She exclaims this with a relief that surprises me. "Isn't it something how in this cautious society they would put you through all that? Really—when they got everything they wanted in the excision?"

"Well . . ."

"No—really. I'm sure they got it all when they did the excision. They just want to be cautious . . . well . . . really, in the excision, they got everything, there really was nothing left to get rid of."

She's motioning to her own chest now as she's speaking, has her hands flat against her breasts in the way I've seen many women pose once we get talking about the cancer. Nobody seems to realize they're doing this, but I notice and it's fascinating. For this friend, I think any fear of my having a "real" problem has become her own. If it could happen to me, it could happen to her. And then, I'm sure, it indeed would be real.

✌︎✍︎

At the hospital, the valet—a new guy—tells me that I can park in the lot but if I have a problem finding a space they can take care of the car for me. He's very polite. I thank him. I also know better than he does where all the spots are, even when all the marked ones are gone and it appears there is no room left. If you go along the far curb, one car can fit by the end. Across from that, another two, one next to the other. Today, I back the car into one of the extra ones. I put on the Walkman earphones, insert *Songs for a Lead-Lined Room* and walk to the entrance. I see the cheery female valet over there. I don't want to be like I was with Luz, to whom I never said a proper goodbye and to whom I still wish I'd apologized for not being able to look at her the first days— whether or not she noticed that, whether or not it meant anything to her. This one valet has come to mean a warm welcome to a place that is no thrill to visit daily. I want to tell her that. So I follow her to the little white valet headquarters hut, where the key rings hang neatly, paperwork is done, tips counted. When she emerges, I tell her that I just wanted to say I've been coming here for seven weeks and it's not been easy—"It probably wasn't," she throws in—and I say that of all the people in this crew she is the nicest and the cheeriest and when I see her face as I drive up it is a good moment. She nods, and thanks me, and don't know what else to say, so I leave. I walk through the doors tha part magically, take a right at the sign that warns you not to bring in balloons and past the warning to stay out if you have the flu, past an extra sign that announces that the baby shop is going to have a 25-percent-off sale just for hospital employees, probably none of whom are babies.

I take the right. Two special needs guys are in front of me. They are lost and ask a man at the elevators how to find Centennial, which is the main entrance at the other end of the hospital, and the man at the elevators says, come with me, which is a nice thing because even if you did not have the challenges of special needs it would take you all day to find your way across this building unassisted. I pass them. I see some familiar workers' faces. I kick up the Walkman's volume. The song about the sky, ocean noises and stones rolling with the tide. I want to be there. Not passing under yet another sign for radiation oncology. The big round letters. The long hall. The horror-movie litany: you have this, you have this. There's my destination, and, in front of me, a guy who looks in fine shape—a doctor yet—hits the button so that both doors to the department, both of them open, as if he needed to push a bed through. He strolls in, hands unoccupied. I follow. I say hi to Angela. Angela says, "Good afternoon, Miss Shea." I get a drink of water from the bubbler. I walk down the hall. I take a gown from the cabinet. The old Puerto Rican lady is in a cubicle with her daughter helping her disrobe. She waves at me through a gap in the curtain. I wave back. I put on my own uniform—the gown, sweatshirt, Walkman—and I go to wait.

∽∾∾∾

There is only Carvella and me, then the old Puerto Rican lady and her daughter, and another woman somehow related to the pair. Carvella chides me—my last day and she has to wait until tomorrow for that thrill. She tells me about having fluid removed from her surgery site, how this will be her third or so time having that done since August. She asked the doctor if he could teach her how to do it herself, he said no, and we figure they would lose money if patients started doing all their own procedures. The technician calls for Carvella, who stands and comes over to hug me, to wish me luck, then she's gone. The three Puerto Rican ladies regard me with nodding heads. I blurt out that it's my last day, the same way I felt I had to tell that woman in the tower that I was carrying a bird back to its world. The old lady turns for a translation. I took two years and I can't remember a word of Spanish now. But one comes to me: finito. Though I don't say it.

The daughter lady asks me: "What you have?" So I tell her. And she says, "Oh I don't have that, but I have fatty ones," and she points to her chest just in case I can't see that. She tells me, "I don't care, as long as there's nothing wrong with them. If they told me I had what she had"—here she nods toward the old lady, who is smiling and nodding as well—"I'd just fall apart. Fall apart. Her? She doesn't care. They won't do surgery—she's too old. She's just in here to, to, make it smaller. They can't do anything other than that. But she doesn't care. She just doesn't worry about things." Next to her, the old lady is nodding again, and she too looks as if she has not one single concern.

The second lady's mother is another story, and I am told that "she always says she has something wrong. 'Oh, this hurts'; 'I have this.' People in the family take time from work to take her to the doctor's, and the local specialists—no good for her. She wants to go far. To Boston. To Hartford. People have to lose work just because she thinks she has a pain. Now she thinks she has a brain tumor and she's gonna die. She knows she does. That's what she says. I say, 'If you know, then you know. Why do you want a doctor to tell you?' She says she needs them to tell her. She's eighty-seven. Had cataracts. I told her to leave them alone. She says she wants the surgery. They do it. Now she can't see out of one eye. She cries that she can't see. I say, 'I told you not to have that done.'"

Then she moves on and tells me about her mother's sister, her aunt. Just as bad. Eighty-five. "The two of them put together drive the family crazy," she says.

There are more relatives, I'm sure, but it is my turn so I won't hear about the rest of them. In the room, one of the other technicians says she remembers marking me for the first machine. "It seems like you just started," she says, something I cannot agree with.

I get on the table and they ask if I brought "Pomp and Circumstance" on the Walkman. I ask, how about the "Hallelujah Chorus." Either one would do, they say. "Both of them make me cry," says one. "I cry at everything. My daughter voted for the first time the other day, I saw her go into the booth, I cried." I tell her she should have cried only if the daughter had voted Republican. The woman stops and frowns, "Now, now. . . ."

They leave the room and I'm there alone with the smiley face on the ceiling and the circling Pooh and the constellations on the wall, Ursa Major and Minor. Buzz, whir, refrigerator noise, it's over. That simple.

The two women return and they pull the machine away and tell me I'm free to go. But not before I get my diploma. The one named Lucy gives it to me. It's a rolled-up thing with a blue ribbon encircling it. I say they have to be kidding, they say no, everybody gets this. And I remember the man in the waiting room the first day I was here, proud about this. I unroll my copy and look at the staffers' names, not the sentiment. Nothing registers with me right then. Later, I'll examine it, will see the confetti stars and ribbons in color and the big words: "Congratulations on completing your course of radiation therapy. We were happy to be a part of your care and treatment."

There are the signatures of Mary Ann and Linda and Michell and Annette who's off this big day. Nancy. Carole. Melissa. Jenni. I didn't know that many people worked here. The two women are standing in front of me and I start my story, how it's been since March and that's why I can't believe this even now, here in November.

"Two thousand was bad, two thousand and one will be better," Lucy tells me sincerely, and each of them hugs me and wishes me well. I walk out, past the Disney posters and into the hallway and there's

Wendy, who asks me to her office. She signs the diploma because she hadn't yet. As she does, I see a full list of patients on her computer screen, all bearing problems she will try to assist with or at least listen to. My name was on there once. I still have my problems in my own head. But the edges are off them, thanks to her, and to time. I also know what the problems look like now, the general forms of them at least, rather than seeing them in some shape so foreign there isn't even a name invented for them. Another hug, a goodbye to the guru, and I leave the little office where I've deposited so many of my feelings and mind-debris that I maybe should vacuum here, too. At the reception-ist's window, I thank Angela and say goodbye and she replies, "Good-bye, Miss Shea." On the television, a couple on *General Hospital* is planning their marriage, and the same two women who were watching the Halloween show are there in the chairs, rapt. I walk out the door of radiation oncology. My first foot forward is my left. Way back when, in normal life, I would take this as bad luck. I'm a righty, I intention-ally start most things on the right, with the right, to the right. But this problem I have is on my left. This thing I have, this thing, this condi-tion, this illness, this sickness. You know, your problem, your, your cancer. That is on my left. So maybe left will be my new way to go.

≋≋

I start the Walkman and the song about the sky and the ocean is up, the surf noises and the catching the bus and starting the magic journey, a mighty drama unfolding so slowly—the word is whispered: "slowly." But I'm walking quickly. Past housekeeping and the elevators, the right down the wide deserted hall. Past the doors for the couriers, the birth certificates, and then my elevator, above me the words RADIATION ON-COLOGY, but let them be there repeating themselves as much as they want to—I am not looking this time. And hope I won't have to see them ever again. Now my gaze is straight on, then right, the turn toward the hall heading to wound care and hyperbaric chamber, a left at the multi-cultural clay people, into the lobby and past the flu-warning sign, a left through the mix of new mothers and past the baby gift shop with its infant Halloween costumes on sale now at 35 percent off. Foot—not sure which, but it doesn't matter—on the mat that opens the door and then I am outside, passing the valets and their red jackets, down the sidewalk, cutting through the lot and opening my car door. Across the way, a young mother is unfolding a tiny, tiny wheelchair and then she goes back into her van for a little toddler who gets seated into that, and they roll from my view. I sit in the car and there is no noise. No whoosh. No nothing. I turn the key. I put the car in gear. Everything around me moves. I am out of the tower. Somebody, something, came along and rescued me. Carried me out and is letting me go.

The scarf is below me. I pick my feet from it. I'm a brown creeper no longer creeping, instead flying off to the beat of the waves. Solitary. Moving up the hill in undulating wavy motions like the shapes you draw to make the sea, a looping pattern that takes me from the parking lot onto Chestnut Street and above the brownish trees and across the road and far off in the direction of the northeast, over the great lovely wooded country that gives the sacred illusion that nobody lives here. You can watch until you're sure you can see me no longer, until it almost is painful to stare and be certain that the dot that I am now is gone from this place and soaring over the land of hurt and healing, attempt and failure and prized success, of a missing girl and a dead man, where everybody has their stories, and their stuff, and where things happen good and bad, dark and light, balance attempted and some blessed times achieved. Below me is as much yin and yang as if the symbol were tattooed across the planet. This, here, this is where I've been. This is where I am. This is where I live.

# ☙ Epilogue ☙

It's 6:30 A.M., middle of the week, middle of July 2001. I am pulling my suitcase through the quiet little airport in Madison, Wisconsin. And there is Molly Bish.

On the cover of *People*.

The gift shop tended by the yawning clerk displays a big row of the magazines, each of them repeating the same image against a black background, the largest picture being pensive missing intern Chandra Levy, and the three smaller photos featuring her sisters' fate: one young woman who never showed up for lunch with her father; another who was last seen on a cruise ship; and, at the far left, the smiling blonde teenager who disappeared from her lifeguard post. All of them frozen, as the cliché goes, "in happier times," and displayed there under the headline of "Vanished."

It's a year and month since Molly's disappeared, a year and month since I was diagnosed. Molly Bish was missing at that time, and has yet to be seen. Around the same time, I vanished in a way as well. Oh, you certainly could have seen me, touched me, treated me, but the "me" I always was changed with the news that I had cancer. I'm sitting in Cindy's kitchen on a Sunday during the winter, she's chopping vegetables and she turns to me and out of nowhere says, "You know that thing about you wanting your old life back?" And I nod yeah, what about it? "Well," she says, "you might as well forget that." And she's right. I'm not going to be the person I was before last year, and who I will be now, with the insights and experiences that have knocked into me and added to me, remains to be seen. But I'm on some kind of track, one that has me strong enough, physically and mentally, to resume my work and take on what I'm doing when I spot the *People* magazine and Molly—flying from city to city for two weeks and nearly every night getting up in front of a crowd of people to promote my newest novel. "What will your next book be about?" I always get that question. This time I respond, "My having breast cancer." And I get the look.

At one point in my travels I meet a woman from France who wants to know about the cancer, and after listening she concludes in her great little accent, "Life must be so beautiful to you now, no?"

I say sort of, and she cocks her head and frowns as she figures out what that means. I say, it's kind of like Thanksgiving, which came just after my treatments ended. So many people told me I was going to have the best holiday ever, so much to be thankful for. But my head was still spinning. I went to my in-laws for the meal and on the way back asked Tommy to stop the car at the big decorated Portuguese cemetery I'd passed every day on the way to the hospital. A childhood friend who'd battled breast cancer for eight years had just been buried there. We stepped through the snow in the newer part of the cemetery and finally found her grave, which was decorated with a ceramic Christmas tree and a card that would mark her place until a stone could be erected. She was born a year after I was, 1959. I stood there not knowing the feelings crawling through me, and when I identified one I shoved away the selfish gratitude that it was not me buried there. That was why I was thankful. That I was not in a cemetery.

≈∂⊂≈

I muddled through the next few months in what I've since learned is called the "now what?" period. You are done with surgery, treatment, the daily checks by health professionals. Now what? Nobody knows. You are turned out into the big meadow of the world to fend for yourself. Someone asked me, so what do you do now? And I said, you just go day to day hoping you don't get anything again. They said goodbye shortly after my answer. Most people don't want to know what you are really thinking. They want it to be what I myself would have wanted: a fast and mindless TV show. The problem of cancer is introduced in the Movie of the Week, and by the end of the two hours, just before the 11 P.M. news, there is the happy conclusion. A life saved in Hollywood fashion after a brave battle by a patient who thought only of others when she was at her worst. In grade school we read the paperback of *Brian's Song,* then watched it on TV. James Caan looked spectacular as he lay dying. He gritted his teeth and winced, "Jeezus God I'm trying" when asked how he was. He looked fantastic to the end. Was funny. Tried hard. Buoyed his wife. Cajoled his pals. Made you understand why at the end of the film his best friend would announce to the world, "I luuuuuuv Brian Piccolo." I wasn't funny, I didn't try, I didn't look so fantastic. I scrambled upstairs when people came by. Pushed away my husband to the point where he was so small I could hardly see him. Tried the patience of those who'd known me the longest. It wasn't pretty, or telegenic, or what I would have predicted if I'd ever thought of how I'd be as a patient. But who imagines that picture ahead of time? There are no books titled *This Is How to Act When You Get Sick,* just as there are no books that prepare loved ones for what they'll be feeling. No-six-weeks-for-twenty-five dollars courses on the correct steps, timing, rhythm so we can all look good on the big day. We learn as we go. We might not act in the most popular manner, but we should be allowed to make our own choices. To proceed by instinct. Do what we need to do. If somebody who is sick can't think of themselves at this edge-of-the-cliff point in their travels, "What's it gonna take?"

∽∾

One year after my surgery I still find myself feeling guilty. As if I somehow brought on the cancer that resulted in confusion and pain for people I love. I can be harsh with myself, can still go between that and back to feeling sorry for me me me—whoever that "me" is now. I do feel like a different person. Some of the pastimes and people that I used to love or enjoy don't hold meaning for me any longer. My body has returned, my strength, but something I can't name is missing. There is a Native American belief about the soul having to catch up with the body after a long journey is made. That makes sense to me. I feel I'm standing at the station looking down the tracks and waiting for the train that is carrying the inside of me. The engine will pull up in a big cloud of warm steam and the essence of me will jump from the door into my arms and my center and click in like the final puzzle piece you needed out of the thousand in the box. And I will feel whole.

But, as the wise woman said, I probably should forget about that. My soul will arrive when it arrives. Waiting won't hasten its trip. Rather than tap my foot at the railway platform, I should make my way in this current state and find out who I am now with this new knowledge of life. I've learned a lot. But I'm not yet one of the people who can say they are grateful for the cancer that taught them so much—I'm not rushing to fill in the magazine's "I had cancer and then . . ." blank. Maybe in time I will be, though—I can already see it was a good kick in the ass to work on my problem areas: self-esteem and self-love, codependency, the bigger picture. You are here for something, I think. And I'm still here. Easily, what I am writing here could have had a less than happy ending. Easily, I could not be here to write it.

I am no longer obsessed by the "why" of my cancer—why did I get it, why me? Now I think very often of what I am supposed to do with it. What part will it play as I leave the country of illness and get back on my track? I try not to have that kettle boiling away on the front burner all day. I push it to the back where it can simmer and, maybe in time, provide its own answer subtly and uniquely. In the meantime I m working my way along my days, trying to be patient and loving with myself and with those who showed me so much compassion when I needed it but at the same time couldn't receive it. I'm restarting the new novel, editing this very book, and also finishing up promotion for the last and one night I'm doing a reading at my town library and look up to find that the next person waiting to have her book signed is Magdalen Bish.

She wears denim overalls pinned with the PRAY FOR MOLLY badge. Her earrings are dragonflies, which the family has chosen as the beautiful and airy symbol of their still-missing daughter. She's smiling, telling me how she and her husband love my books. I start to babble, how many times I've thought of Molly, of her family, how bad I felt in November when I signed three books to donate to the raffle at the "Swish for Bish" basketball tournament fundraiser but couldn't get my act together enough to get off my bed and drive the one mile to deliver them to the school. "I wanted to do something," I say, as so many people must say to her, and then my babble fades away as I have no excuse that wouldn't be embarrassing. This woman's daughter has disappeared one year and one month ago this very day, yet she can find the desire and energy to attend something like a bookreading on a Friday evening. I had been done with my treatments and really not doing much of anything, yet was unable to drive down the street. Magdalen waves away any concern. "We do what we can do," she tells me tenderly, then she opens her copy and asks that I sign it "To Babci," which is Polish for grandmother, another thing Magdalen Bish is and is proud to be called. I do as she asks and I give her what has to be her millionth hug in the past year and a month, and she slips into a loud crowd of good-natured friends and they go off to dinner and another reader takes her place in the line in front of me, the night moves on, is over, and then just as you'd hope if you were in the headspace to be back to hoping again, here comes another day and, as unpredictably frightening as days can be, there is just as much yin-yang chance that they might just hold something good.

On one of my days I find myself in Ireland. For real, not just on the headphones. I'm headed to the ocean, intending to walk as far as I can in that direction before surrendering to a bus stop. There is a pack on my back and boots on my feet, the wide sky overhead, the ocean to my right. And, in my head, a caution from a friend who reminded me to keep safe. I know to do that, but he insists, no hitching—which I don't do—and stay on the path—which I will—as I shrug him off and he reminds me of life's realities, things outside your body that can cause harm: bad people who make victims of women. "Nothing's going to happen to me," I say reassuringly, a bit annoyed at the lecture, raring to get on my way, to put one foot in front of the other and get somewhere I want to be.

The day is fair and clear and I follow the road outside the city, using a footpath that puts a wide buffer of grass and wildflowers between me and the traffic. Summer is starting, a too-short season of warmth and sun, and vacationers whiz past in great numbers. Farther from the city, the road forks, gets quieter, leads into farmland and woods. The footpath has the same idea, and takes me into a world of its own—parallel to the road but farther from it, angling down a hill and into a glade with bony trees cradling toward one another to form a tunnel. Moss covers bark and gives a fairytale feel. Woodland flowers are dots of white against the green carpet, insects make their various songs, my walking is a silent thing now as the soft ground muffles steps. So, in this wonderland that has me aching for the camera I no longer carry, that is why I see him first, rather than hear his steps as he walks toward me on this path. This same quiet, deserted path that now has parted so much from the road that I can neither hear nor see the cars. Normal day, normal walk, normal life, I'd get ready to say hi. But the seed has been put in my head, and it germinates, sprouts and grows ten feet in the span of two seconds: here is one of those bad people about whom I was warned. And something is going to happen to me.

He's ten feet away, my heart is in a new gear, my pacifist hand jammed into the pocket where I keep the pocket knife that only knows how to cut bread and those scratchy little plastic strings from price-tags. I increase my pace, fix my posture, move with what I hope looks like don't-mess-with-me confidence. The man is tall and muscular and maybe thirty. Where is he coming from? What is he doing out here? Five feet from me now. Howya, he says, and I nod the same. I move faster. Hope he is well behind me now. A few steps and I turn to check. And I do that at the same time he turns to check on me. I run. I am not a runner, I am a walker. Plus I have this pack on, something I don't think to throw off as I head down the path and—shit—now there is a hill. I run up it and now I can hear the whizzing of traffic again. I turn off the path and run to the left, in its direction, through low scrubby bushes and ferns, and trip over roots and fallen branches, over this thing echoing through my head: "I'm gonna get killed, I'm gonna get killed, I'm gonna get killed." I was daydreaming and now I am going to pay.

I don't turn to see how close he is because I don't want to lose sight of my destination, the clearing I can see blue through the shrubbery ahead. I charge smack into it, breathing hard and high and panicky. A wall of brambles grabs me, hooks into my clothes, my skin. I tear with my hands, pull the canes from my pants, raise my leg high and get myself another foot toward—shit again—a fence that is maybe five feet high. I manage another awkward step and the thorns that you would not believe could immobilize a human prevent me from going any far-ther. I suddenly am aware of the pack. I pull it off and with new astro-naut weightlessness I throw myself toward the planks and catch one with a hand, kicking my legs along, and climb, climb, another leg free now, and then a dropped-rock fall over to the other side, where there is clear and blessed safety.

I am slumped on the edge of the highway. Scraped and bleeding, clothing ripped, pack needing retrieval, but me, I am OK. Not grabbed, not murdered, not dead. Alive. I've been tumbled onto the road again. Only, this time when I don't know where I've landed, I am thinking I will be OK.

The fence is my backrest now. I sit and I watch the families driving past only feet from my feet. Curious faces in car windows, a white cow in the field across the way, life going on. I take a crushed and sweat-damp box of raisins from the pocket that holds the knife and I wait to stop breathing so hard. Then I begin to eat.

A nun passes on a bicycle, her black habit flowing back like hair. She raises her hand in a benediction. I raise mine. I'm OK, I'm telling her. Don't help me. I'm OK.

More cars pass. Trucks. Occupants look at me, I look at them. I sit there. I eat my raisins. Open another box. Sit some more. I sit maybe longer than some would. Maybe not as long as others. I eat more raisins than some would. Maybe fewer than others might. But I'm me, and that's what I did after my big scare. And then, after I got that big scare that didn't kill me, I did what I did. What you would do might be entirely different. We do what we can do. And this is what I did, both that day, and with my illness:

When I was ready, and not a moment before, when I felt I'd had enough sitting and looking and resting and thinking and when I thought it was time to start my journey again, only then and not a millisecond sooner, I tended to my wounds and stood up and reached over the wall for my thorn-suspended pack and looked into the dark of the woods where I'd had my fright and then I looked into the light of the world I'd fallen into and I picked a direction and I continued my walk on a road I'd never before been on.

I hoped the destination would be a good one, hoped, hoped, but, really, just was happy to be moving. In the sunshine, past the folding table holding baskets of strawberries for sale, its bored young minder thumbing a Nintendo, past the inlet with the graceful beached dory, past some type of black birds debating in their ash tree. Step by step, one foot in front of the other I moved, the way so long ago I learned. I am learning all over again. God is thinking of me. I am still here. And I walk on.

SOME BOOKS I FOUND HELPFUL:

*The Collected Poems,* by Reynolds Price (Scribner, 1997)

*Dr. Susan Love's Breast Book,* by Susan M. Love and Karen Lindsey (Perseus Book Group, third revised edition, September 2000)

*From This Moment On: A Guide for Those Recently Diagnosed with Cancer,* by Arlene Cotter (Random House, 1999)

*New and Selected Poems,* by Mary Oliver (Beacon Press, 1992)

*Speak the Language of Healing: Living with Breast Cancer without Going to War,* by Susan Kuner, Carol Matzkin Orsborn, Linda Quigley, Karen Leigh Stroup (Conari Press, 1999)

*Your Life in Your Hands,* by Jane A. Plant (St. Martin's Press, 2000)

AND IN THE BACKGROUND WAS:

*Beautiful Wreck of the World,* Willie Nile (River House Records, 2000)

*Crossing Muddy Waters,* John Hiatt (Vanguard, 2000)

*Diamond Mountain Sessions,* Sharon Shannon and Friends (Compass, 2000)

*Holy Smokes,* Suzzy Roche (Red House Records, 1997)

*Largo,* Various Artists (Uni/Mercury Records, 1998)

*New Boots New Shoes,* Seamus Ruttledge (Independent release, 2000, www.sawdoctors.com)

*Same Oul' Town,* The Saw Doctors (Shamtown Records, 1996)

*Sound!* Padraig Stevens (Independent release, 1996, www.sawdoctors.com)

*Tropical Brainstorm,* Kirsty McColl (Instinct Records, 2001)

Anyone having information on the disappearance of Molly Bish should visit www.mollybish.com or should phone the Massachusetts State Police in Warren at 1-800-808-9677.

The following is a list of names invented to protect privacy.
All other names in the book are real.

*Annette*

*Carvella*

*Becky Dobek*

*Jack*

*Tim Kargol*

*Larry*

*Lucy*

*Luz*

*Margaret*

*Stella*

*Mr. and Mrs. Vasquez*

*Wendy*

# 〽️ Acknowledgments 〽️

Shortly after I was diagnosed with breast cancer in July of 2000, Sharon Young suggested that I write about how I was feeling. In the months that followed, Tommy Shea kept reminding me of what Sharon had said. When I finished the journal entries that would become this book, Tanya Barrientos sent me her laptop and Padraig Stevens lent me a place to finish this and to start anew. This book exists because of them.

I also am grateful for help and compassion from Sue O'Hare; Dr. Michael Albert; Dr. Mary Ann Lowen; Kathleen Kelly; the Comprehensive Breast Center and the Radiation Oncology Department of Baystate Medical Center in Springfield, Massachusetts; my book doctor, Elsie Osterman; my agent, John Talbot; Helene Atwan, my editor and the director of Beacon Press; and those, both known and unknown to me, who hoped and prayed.